Foreword

Thank you for choosing "Business Entities for Entrepreneurs & Managers" as a resource for your business venture. Understanding business entities is essential to the effective planning, formation, growth, and continued management of the business ventures. This text provides a straightforward guide for entrepreneurs, managers, and legal practitioners who are not extremely familiar with the key attributes of the most common types of business entity. It covers issues including: formation, location, maintenance, control, authority, liability, compensation, taxation, and funding. It also discusses the use of specific entity types for startup ventures. The text is organized in an easy-to-read, question-and-answer format that breaks down the elements of each business entity into small digestible pieces.

Please understand that this text is not fully comprehensive. There are innumerable attributes that characterize a given business entity; however, this text will provide you with much of the background knowledge of business entities that you will need when making fundamental business decisions. You should consider consulting a legal and accounting professional when facing important decisions concerning your business entity.

I hope you enjoy the text. We welcome commentary and feedback on our product. Please visit our website at www.TheBusinessProfessor.com to view our other texts and free learning resources.

Attribution

I would like to thank Mr. Steven Meier, Esquire of Meir Carr, PC (http://maiercarr.com) for his review and commentary on various portions of this text.

ENTITY

CREATION AND MAINTENANCE OF THE BUSINESS ENTITY

How do you create a business entity?

What form of maintenance is required for a default business entity?

What form of maintenance is required for non-default business entities?

How could a business lose its entity status?

How and why would a plaintiff challenge a business entity status?

CONTINUITY OF THE BUSINESS ENTITY

What types of conduct by business owners can cause the business to dissolve?

OWNERSHIP RIGHTS AND CONTROL OF THE BUSINESS ENTITY

Who really owns the business?

Who has control or authority to run the business?

What should businesses do to reduce issues regarding ownership and control?

COMPENSATION TO BUSINESS OWNERS

How is an owner of a business compensated?

PERSONAL LIABILITY OF BUSINESS OWNERS

What is limited liability?

What is the extent of personal liability protection?

What are the ways that a business entity can lose its liability shield?

How can a business owner do more to protect herself from personal liability?

TAXATION OF BUSINESS ENTITIES

CHAPTER 3: AGENCY LAW & LIABILITY

What is agency law and why is it important in understanding business entities?

Who is a principal?

Who is an agent?

What is an independent contractor and how does it relate to agency law?

How can a non-employee (such as an independent contractor) be an agent of the principal?

Who is a third party and why is the concept important?

What special duties does the agent owe to the principal?

What is vicarious liability?

What is respondeat superior?

When is an employer-principal not liable for the actions of the employee-agent?

What can an employer recover from an employee for acts that make the employer vicariously liable?

When is an employer contractually liable for an agent's Acts?

TALK MORE ABOUT AGENCY

What is actual authority?

What is implied authority?

What is apparent authority?

What is ratification?

CHAPTER 4: TAXATION OF THE OWNER AND BUSINESS ENTITY

What do I need to know about business taxation to effectively understand business entities?

How are individuals taxed on their personal incomes?

How are business entities taxed?

What are payroll and self-employment taxes?

What other special rules apply to how businesses are taxed?

What happens if the business has losses?

What is basis?

What are the basis and at-risk limitations?

What is a passive loss?

How does the IRS determine what is passive and active income or losses?

What happens if the business does not distribute any of the profits to the owners?

CHAPTER 5: THE SOLE PROPRIETORSHIP

How are sole proprietorships created?

Who has ownership and control over a sole proprietorship?

What is the continuity of a sole proprietorship?

What is the personal liability of the sole proprietor?

How is the sole proprietorship taxed?

What are the sole proprietor's other tax reporting obligations?

How does sales and use tax withholding work?

What are the employee and self-employment tax withholding rules?

CHAPTER 6: GENERAL PARTNERSHIPS & JOINT VENTURES

GENERAL PARTNERSHIP (GP)

What is a GP?

What is a GP agreement and why is it important?

What are the important provisions to cover in a partnership agreement?

How is the GP formed?

What other steps should I follow in forming the GP?

Who owns a GP?

Who has control and authority to act on behalf of the GP?

What are the partners' duties to the GP?

What is the business continuity in a GP?

What is a buy-sell agreement and why is it important?

What is the personal liability of the partners?

How are GPs taxed?

How are partners compensated?

What is a special allocation and how does it work?

What is each partner's tax basis?

What happens if the GP wishes to make a distribution when it is not profitable?

What if the partners leave any of the profits in the business, rather than take them out as a distribution?

What happens if the GP suffers losses?

JOINT VENTURES

What is a joint venture?

What are the key difference between the joint venture and the GP?

CHAPTER 7: LIMITED PARTNERSHIPS & OTHER HYBRIDS

LIMITED PARTNERSHIP (LP)

What is a LP?

How are LPs created?

How is the LP maintained?

Who owns the LP?

Who has control and authority in a LP?

What types of activity can the limited partner undertake with respect to the business?

What are the limited partner's rights in the business beyond receiving a percentage of profits?

What is the continuity of a LP?

What personal liability protection does a LP offer?

How is a LP taxed?

Where are LPs most commonly used?

LIMITED LIABILITY PARTNERSHIPS (LLP)

What is a LLP?

How is the LLP created?

Who owns a LLP?

Who controls the LLP?

What is the continuity of the LLP?

What limited liability protection does the LLP offer?

How is a LLP taxed?

When is a LLP used?

LIMITED LIABILITY LIMITED PARTNERSHIPS (LLLP)

What is a LLLP?

How is a LLLP created?

Who owns the LLLP?

Who controls the LLLP?

What is the continuity of the LLLP?

How is the LLLP taxed?

Where is the LLLP commonly used?

What is the personal liability of LLLP partners?

CHAPTER 8: LIMITED LIABILITY COMPANIES

What is a limited liability company (LLC)?

How is a LLC created?

What must be included in the articles of organization?

What are the LLC maintenance requirements?

What is an operating agreement?

How can a business change into an LLC?

Who owns the LLC?

Who has control over the LLC?

How are members of an LLC compensated?

What is the continuity of an LLC?

What limited personal liability protection does the LLC offer?

How can an LLC member lose personal liability protection?

When is an LLC owner personally liable (other than when the court pierces the veil)?

How are LLCs taxed?

Are LLC distributions treated as active or passive income?

What activities affect the owner's basis in the LLC?

CHAPTER 9: CORPORATIONS

What is a corporation?

How is the corporation created?

What is included in the articles of incorporation?

What are the corporate bylaws and why do they matter?

How are corporations maintained?

How do these requirements change for small and closely-held corporations (such as startup ventures)?

Why do many businesses incorporate in Delaware?

Who owns the corporation?

Who has authority or controls the corporation?

What is the authority of shareholders?

What is the authority of the board of directors?

What is the authority of officers?

What is the continuity of the corporation?

What is the extent of limited liability protection in a corporation?

How can a shareholder lose limited liability protection?

How are corporations taxed?

What are the requirements to qualify as an S corporation?

Are there any ways to be a C corporation and avoid double taxation?

PROFESSIONAL CORPORATIONS

What are professional corporations?

STATUTORY-CLOSE CORPORATIONS

What is a statutory-close corporation?

CHAPTER 10: NON-PROFITS

What is a non-profit?

What types of activities qualify for non-profit status?

How is a non-profit formed?

What are the maintenance requirements for non-profits?

Who owns and controls a non-profit?

What is the non-profit continuity?

What profit is a non-profit allowed to make?

What are the limitations on non-profits?

What type of unrelated activities are exempt from taxation?

What limited liability protection does a non-profit offer?

How does a non-profit raise money?

What are the main benefits of organizing as a non-profit?

What are the disadvantages of organizing as a non-profit?

CHAPTER 11: IDENTIFYING THE APPROPRIATE STARTUP ENTITY

THE SOLE PROPRIETORSHIP

What are the primary considerations in carrying on business as a sole proprietorship?

Is a sole proprietorship ever appropriate for a business that sells products?

Is a sole proprietorship appropriate for a business that has employees?

Should a business with a physical business location that is open to the public operate as a sole proprietorship?

Should a business with potential contract liability operate as a sole proprietorship?

PARTNERSHIPS

What are the primary considerations for the GP?

What are the primary considerations for the LP?

What are the considerations for a LLP?

LIMITED LIABILITY COMPANIES

What are the primary considerations for the LLC?

How does the LLC management structure provide benefits for a startup?

What are the primary drawbacks to using an LLC as a startup structure?

When is a LLC tax structure advantageous for startups?

What are the tax disadvantages for a startup to file as an LLC?

CORPORATIONS

What are the primary considerations for startups considering a corporate entity status?

What about the C corporation maintenance requirements?

What are the benefits and detriments of the double tax structure?

What other tax benefits exist for the C corporation?

What other tax detriments exist for the C corporation?

How does the C corporation equity structure benefit the startup?

What about the S corporation?

What tax benefits exist for the S corporation?

What tax detriments exist for the S corporation?

How does the S corporation compare to the LLC as a startup entity?

What about a non-profit entity?

CHAPTER 12: SETTING UP THE BUSINESS ENTITY

What goes into the entity formation process?

What do I file with the state Secretary of State's Office?

What tax documents do I file?

When do I draft the entity governance documents?

What actions do the organizers of a partnership take?

What actions do the organizers of the LLC take?

What actions do the incorporators and initial board of directors of a corporation take?

What actions do the shareholders of the corporation take?

What formal steps should the corporate board take with regard to issuing corporate equity?

What formal steps should the members of a partnership or LLC take with regard to issuing business equity?

What employee and intellectual property matters should the board of directors or officers' address?

How does the corporation secure intellectual property rights?

CHAPTER 13: TAX PLANNING WHEN FUNDING AN ENTITY

CORPORATIONS

What tax issues arise when funding a business entity?

Does a shareholder incur a tax liability when transferring property to a corporation in exchange for equity?

Does a corporation incur a tax liability when receiving property in exchange for equity?

What are the requirements to defer tax liability when transferring property to a corporation?

Can shareholder lose the tax deferment benefit when transferring property to a corporation?

What is the result if the shareholder receives some form of value in addition to corporate shares?

What is the shareholder's basis in the stock following the transfer?

What is the corporation's basis in the property following the transfer?

What happens if the corporation assumes shareholder debt associated with the transferred property?

What happens if the equity received by the shareholder is in exchange for services to the corporation?

How can a shareholder elect to immediately recognize as income shares that are subject to a risk of forfeiture?

PARTNERSHIP - TAXED ENTITIES

What is the tax liability of the partnership when property is transferred to the entity in exchange for an ownership interest?

What are the requirements for an exemption from the recognition of gains in an IRC Section 721 transaction?

What is the partner's basis in the ownership interest following the transfer?

What is the partnership's basis in the property following the transfer?

What is the result if a partner receives some form of value in addition to an ownership interest?

What happens if the partnership assumes shareholder debt associated with the transferred property?

What happens if the partner contributes property to the partnership with gain that is later sold by the partnership?

What happens if property contributed to the partnership is later distributed to other partners?

How do partnerships allocate losses on the sale of property with a built-in-gain?

What happens if the equity received by the partner is in exchange for services to the partnership?

CHAPTER 14: CONVERTING ENTITIES

What is the process to convert from one entity status to another?

What are the options in converting from a partnership or LLC (partnership) to a corporate entity status?

Do partners recognize any gain or loss in the conversion from a partnership to a corporate entity?

Does the partnership recognize any gain or loss in the conversion from a partnership to a corporate entity?

What will be the partner's basis in the new corporation?

What is the new corporation's basis in assets contributed by the partners or partnership?

What does it take to convert from S to C corporation status?

What are the tax consequences of converting from S to C corporation status?

What does it take to convert from C corporation status to a partnership or LLC?

What does it take to convert from C to S corporation status?

When is the S election effective?

What are the tax consequences when converting from C to S corporation status?

CHAPTER 15: WHEN TO INCORPORATE

How can incorporating early help avoid disputes with other founders?

When should I incorporate to limit personal liability?

Should I incorporate before hiring employees?

How does timing affect business intellectual property?

How does timing affect the tax basis for founder ownership interest?

How does incorporating early in the life of the startup facilitate equity financing?

What other considerations on timing are important when incorporating?

CHAPTER 16: IN WHICH STATE TO INCORPORATE

Why do companies incorporate in Delaware?

What are Delaware's formation and maintenance advantages?

What are the advantages of Delaware's chancery courts and body of corporate law?

How are Delaware laws favorable to corporations?

What type of governance requirements attracts startups?

Do investors prefer Delaware corporations?

What are the downsides of incorporating in Delaware?

Why do some businesses incorporate in the Cayman Islands (or other tax haven localities)?

CHAPTER 17: MULTI-STATE BUSINESSES

What happens when a business wants to do business in more than one state?

What constitutes "doing business" within a state?

What happens if the laws of a state in which you wish to do business are different from the laws of the home state?

How similar are each state's business laws?

How are multi-state businesses taxed?

How are multi-state businesses exposed to increased potential liability?

Closing Remarks

CHAPTER 1: AN OVERVIEW OF BUSINESS ENTITIES

INTRODUCTION

Why is studying business entities important?

As entrepreneurs and managers, understanding the characteristics of each type of business entity will improve your proficiency and overall professional competency. Entrepreneurs and managers seek to organize their businesses to maximize productivity and opportunities. While the entrepreneur must choose a business entity, the manager must be aware of how another's entity status will affect any transaction or relationship with her business. In summary, the manager will want to understand the other businesses' ownership structure, organizational structure, potential liability, priority of payment, etc.; further, a business owner needs to be familiar with the type and characteristics of business entities with which she is doing business. This text provides you with the information necessary to feel confident in choosing an entity form for your business, operating within your chosen entity form, and undertaking business transactions with various entity types.

STATE LAW AND BUSINESS ENTITIES

From where do business entities originate?

Before diving into the characteristics of the major business entity types, it is important to understand the legal basis or genesis of business entities. Business entities exist by virtue of state law. Each individual state passes its own substantive and procedural laws regarding business entities. A business may carry on as a registered foreign entity in multiple states, but the business will have one home state or state of formation.

- *Example*: A business may incorporate in Delaware and carry out the majority of its business activity in other states. This situation reflects the business's choice to avail itself of the laws of Delaware for organization, litigation, and other procedural and substantive law reasons.

CLOSELY-HELD AND PUBLICLY-HELD ENTITIES

What is the difference between a closely-held and a publicly-held company?

Business entities are often categorized as either closely-held or publicly-held. This distinction is not a separate type of business entity, but rather a classification or defining characteristic of a given business. Generally, the distinction between the two classifications concerns the number of business owners and whether the equity ownership is sold on a public exchange.

A closely-held business, as the name implies, is held by a smaller or more closely related group of individuals. It is often thought of as a smaller business, such as a mom-and-pop or family business. In truth, however, the closely-held status has little to do with the size or revenue of the business; rather, it simply means that the business is not widely owned by numerous, unrelated people. Another characteristic of the closely-held entity is that it is not traded on a public market.

- *Note*: A closely-held business is a private business. The inverse, however, is not necessarily true. Private business entities do not have to be closely held. Some private businesses (i.e., those not traded on public exchanges) are widely held by a large number of shareholders.

The opposite of a closely-held business is a publicly traded company. A publicly-held or publicly-traded company is held, or capable of being held, by a large number of unrelated people. Any business that is traded on a public exchange is a publicly-held business.

- *Note*: Be careful in assuming that a publicly held business is a corporation. These entities are commonly corporations, but there are examples of limited partnerships and other unique entity types that are publicly traded.

SELECTING A BUSINESS ENTITY STATUS OR ORGANIZATIONAL FORM

What factors should one consider in selecting a business entity form?

Determining what business entity form is most suitable for your business is a subjective determination. The decision will vary depending on the characteristics of the business venture and the nature and intentions of the entrepreneur. There are numerous common considerations that anyone choosing a form of business entity should understand prior to making that decision. Also, the best way to acquire a base understanding of each business entity type and the characteristics that make it unique is to review the determinants for choosing a particular type of entity. Below are the major considerations when choosing a business entity:

- The effort associated with forming and maintaining the entity;
- The continuity or stability of the organization upon given occurrences;
- The ownership rights and control of those involved with the business;
- The compensation and division of profits among business owners;
- The potential for personal liability of those involved with the business; and
- The taxation of the organization's earnings and its distribution of profits to the owners.

This list is certainly not exhaustive. Throughout this text, we include various other considerations that are important in understanding and choosing a business entity.

AGENCY LAW AND BUSINESS ENTITIES

Why is agency law important for business entities?

Agency law concerns the relationship between a business and its agents. Particularly, agency law provides many of the rules concerning who can act on behalf of the business. Perhaps most importantly, agency law governs who can act on behalf of the business. An agent acting on behalf of a business may subject the business to liability in both contract and tort.

How does agency law affect a business's liability for business contracts?

Anyone acting on behalf of the business is an agent. Under agency law, all agents have a certain degree of authority to subject the business entity to liability. Liability generally comes in the form of contract (debts and obligations) and tort (civil liability for the intentional or negligent conduct of employees). As such, understanding the basics of agency law is essential for entrepreneurs and managers of business entities.

How does agency law affect civil lawsuits against a business?

A common refrain ascribed to plaintiff's attorneys is, "Look for the deep pockets." This means that, in any civil action, the plaintiff will seek to identify possible defendants with sufficient resources to compensate for any injuries suffered. Insurance companies and businesses are prime targets. Business entities cannot act on their own behalf; rather, they carry on operations through the actions of the owners and managers of the business.

BUSINESS TAXATION AND ENTITY FORM

What important business tax considerations go into understanding business entities?

Business taxation is a complicated issue. This text examines the primary, business-entity-specific, tax considerations for each entity type. We further discuss pass-through taxation, double taxation, at-risk rules, passive and active income or loss, and basis issues.

REVIEWING THE BUSINESS ENTITIES

What are the main types of business entities?

Each state recognizes its own types of business entity. There are, however, several common business types in all or nearly all of the states. This text reviews the following business entity types:

- Sole Proprietorships
- Partnerships (General, Limited, Limited Liability, and Joint Ventures)
- Limited Liability Companies (LLCs)
- Corporations (S corp, C corp, and other specialty corporate forms)

How do non-profits fit within the business entity regime?

Non-profit entities are generally corporate entities that have a special purpose that qualifies for tax-exempt status from the federal and state government. Some states have separate non-profit, entity forms, while other states recognize non-profits under other established entity forms, such as a corporation.

INFORMATION NECESSARY FOR ENTREPRENEURS

What are the entrepreneurship-specific considerations in choosing an entity status?

Another notable consideration for entrepreneurs or members of growth-based startups is the ability to seek and receive equity funding from outside investors. Each business entity has its limitations with regard to the formalities that exist in selling or transferring an ownership interest in the entity. The form of business entity and organization can also affect the interest of potential outside investors. In any event, a business structure may require significant modifications prior to seeking any outside investment.

CHAPTER 2: CONSIDERATIONS IN CHOOSING A BUSINESS ENTITY

Throughout this text, we will deal with each of the following primary considerations in choosing a business entity.

- The effort associated with forming and maintaining the entity;
- The continuity or stability of the organization upon given occurrences;
- The ownership rights and control of those involved with the business;
- The compensation and division of profits among business owners;
- The potential for personal liability of those involved with the business; and
- The taxation of the organization's earnings and its distribution of profits to the owners.

Each consideration is discussed generally in this chapter. Later chapters discuss these considerations in the context of individual business entity types.

CREATION AND MAINTENANCE OF THE BUSINESS ENTITY

Creation and maintenance are summarized as the administrative steps associated with starting and carrying on business as a given entity form. It entails the process of filing documents, holding meetings, maintaining records, observing formalities, and reporting necessary information to regulators. The requirements for starting a business vary considerably between entity types. Below, we introduce these requirements by splitting them into the creation stage and the maintenance stage.

How do you create a business entity?

Creation of a business entity is the legal or procedural steps that one must undertake to bring the business entity into existence. There is a general dichotomy in the process or steps required to form a business entity. Some business entities require a formal filing process through the Secretary of State's office. Other business entities may arise by default without any formal procedural undertaking by the founder.

Two main types of business entities arise by default, the sole proprietorship and the general partnership. Either of these may arise simply by the parties undertaking some business activity with the intention of generating revenue or making a profit. The only requirement beyond the physical activity of the founders is the subjective intent of the partners with regard to the responsibilities of each party and the allocation of proceeds (or losses) as they arise.

- *Note*: Default entities may still have organizational documents. For example, partners often use partnership agreements to allocate rights and responsibilities among the partners. While the partnership forms by default, the internal relationships, business purpose, operations, and dissolution are often controlled by internal agreement.

All other business entity types arise pursuant to the filing of documents of organization in accordance with the procedural rules adopted by the state of organization. The amount of information and type of document(s) required will vary between states and depend on the type of entity. The general requirements for each business entity type are discussed along with that business entity.

What form of maintenance is required for a default business entity?

Generally, default business entities require little or no maintenance to continue on as a business entity. These businesses arise simply through the conduct of those involved and do not involve the formalized procedure for maintaining their operating status.

- *Note*: While there are few formal maintenance requirements for default entities, there are still numerous tax formalities to follow. The lack of formal maintenance requirements associated with default entities often causes the owners to fail to follow other business formalities. Be careful of this, as failing to follow required formalities could lead to civil or criminal penalties for the business and owners. We will discuss the tax filing requirements in greater detail in later chapters.

What form of maintenance is required for non-default business entities?

Businesses entities that require formal procedures to organize also require formalized maintenance procedures. At the most basic level, these entities require the owners to file statements each year (along with annual fees) with the Secretary of State's office, to hold business meetings, to maintain records, and to report information to regulatory authorities. The state may require that an entity maintain certain records, such as meeting minutes and resolutions, ownership logs, capital accounts, financial statements, etc. The federal government may require that business entities file specific information related to taxation or securities issuances.

- *Note*: Business managers should be cautious when entering into transactions or business relationships with new and small businesses. In certain situations, contracts should contain conditions requiring proof of business entity status and maintenance. In long-term relationships, a supplier or customer that fails to comply with organizational maintenance requirements can be an external or operational threat to a business.

State and reporting requirements can also be industry specific or based upon the company's size or status as privately or publicly-held.

How could a business lose its entity status?

Failing to complete the registration process may cause a business entity registration to fail. Failing to adhere to the state's maintenance requirements can lead to the Secretary of State dissolving a business entity. Lastly, a business entity status is always subject to challenge by plaintiffs bringing an action against the business.

How and why would a plaintiff challenge a business entity status?

This situation arises in business entities that offer limited liability protection to any or all of the business owners. A plaintiff may attack the validity of a business entity in an attempt to subject the owner(s) of the business to personal liability. The plaintiff will argue that the owner of the business failed to follow certain organizational formalities and that the entity is a sham or thin veil for the owners of the business. The plaintiff seeks to "pierce the corporate veil" to hold the business owner personally liable in the action.

The court will review several factors to determine whether the business owner should be afforded protection from personal liability. Under the "alter ego theory," if the owners of a business entity use the business as a shell to protect against liability, then the business entity status will be disregarded. Restated, the business entity would be unified with the business owner, and personal liability protection will be lost.

- *Note*: Maintaining corporate formalities and keeping personal and business assets separate are keys to maintaining the limited liability protection afforded by a business entity. Intermingling personal and business assets is generally the most important consideration in determining whether the court will pierce the corporate veil and attribute personal liability.

CONTINUITY OF THE BUSINESS ENTITY

What types of conduct by business owners can cause the business to dissolve?

This question regards the issue of continuity. The continuity of the business entity concerns the effect on the business of a major change in the ownership and organization structure. Entrepreneurs want to be secure in the stability and durability of the organization if or when an owner leaves the business. Managers are concerned with the stability of customers and suppliers and should make certain that changes in ownership or structure do not have unintended consequences on the business operations.

- *Note*: The primary change affecting the status of a business entity is the death or dissociation of an owner. In some instances this occurrence may be grounds for the dissolution of the business. Another dissolution event may arise through a limitation on the transfer of ownership by any individual in the business. Such a scenario may effectively dissolve the business if one individual wishes to liquidate her interest.

OWNERSHIP RIGHTS AND CONTROL OF THE BUSINESS ENTITY

Who really owns the business?

Ownership in a business, at first glance, seems to be a straightforward issue. When forming a new business, however, the ownership status of those involved in the business can give rise to dispute. This concern is very important for new businesses operating as default entities. Further, some businesses have multiple classes of owners or ownership interests. Understanding the rights of each class of owner requires an understanding of the entities internal governance and structure.

- *Example*: In 2004, Mark Zuckerberg, along with several other individuals, began a social media-based business. Numerous individuals were involved in the business during the development phase. These individuals had poorly defined roles within the business both before and after the business filed for business entity status. The initial failure to formally document ownership interests in the business later gave rise to disputes between the early members. This scenario serves to demonstrate the confusion that arises when ownership interests are not formally established at the outset.

Who has control or authority to run the business?

Managerial control is one of the more complex and liability prone issues surrounding the formation of a business. Each type of business entity, by operation of law, attributes a given level of control to the managers of the business. In many cases the owners and managers of the business are the same people. This relationship becomes convoluted when there are owners who act as managers of the business and others who do not.

- *Example*: Larry, Moe, and Curly form an S corporation. Each is a shareholder and holds an equal percentage of ownership. Each holds a seat on the corporate board and serves as a corporate officer. This relationship requires discipline in that Larry, Moe, and Curly must be careful to take and document actions in accordance with corporate formalities attributable to each position. This includes documenting actions as a shareholder and director by vote in the appropriate forum.

- *Note*: The issue of overlapping ownership and control becomes increasingly important in closely-held business entities. These entities often have owners who also act as managers and others who do not. This raises the concern over who has authority to make decisions and act on behalf of the business.

What should businesses do to reduce issues regarding ownership and control?

Business owners should undertake procedures to outline the role and authority of each member of the business. This is normally done within the business's organizational documents. The title attributable to any owner affects the level of control and authority that she has. Failure to follow procedures to document the authority and control within the business can result in a default level of control or authority in a member of the business that is undesirable to the other owners. Further, a lack of formalized organizational structure can cause internal disputes that affect the operational efficiency of the business.

- *Note*: This issue can be very important regarding issues of business and owner liability. The role of a member entails some level of authority to bind the business in contract. A manager who steps outside of her authority in dealing with third parties may bind the business and the other business owners through their actions. Further, the actions of an individual manager may subject the business, and potentially the other owners, to liability in tort.

COMPENSATION TO BUSINESS OWNERS

How is an owner of a business compensated?

The method of allowable compensation to owners varies between business entities and the role of the owner in the business. Some entities allow for special allocation of business profits between owners. These entities may allow for an owner who acts as an employee to draw a salary from the business, where other entity forms do not. We discuss this issue with regard to each business entity in the following chapters.

- *Note:* The manner of compensation affects how the owner is taxed on business profits. As such, the entity form can allow for or eliminate tax advantages for owners. This is a primary concern for investors in the business.

PERSONAL LIABILITY OF BUSINESS OWNERS

What is limited liability?

Some business entities offer limited liability to owners. This means that the owner is protected from being held personally liable for the debts (contracts) or tortious conduct of the business. Restated, the owner of the business does not risk losing her personal assets for debts created or tortious activity committed by the business or its owners.

- *Example*: The owner of an LLC has two employees who deliver goods to customers. One of the employees accidentally crashes the company vehicle into a pedestrian. The pedestrian can sue the negligent driver and the LLC for damages. The driver may be personally liable for his negligent driving. The LLC may be vicariously liable for the employee's tortious act, since it was committed when the employee was acting in furtherance of the business's operations. The owner's personal assets, however, may be protected from the reach of the plaintiff.

What is the extent of personal liability protection?

The liability protections afforded an owner when doing business as a separate entity is limited. Individuals are always potentially personally liable for their own tortious conduct. In general, liability for the owner or manager of a business comes in two forms, liability for business contracts and liability for business torts. Carrying on as a business entity with limited liability protection may shield the owner from liability on contracts or liability for the tortious actions of those working in or on behalf of the business.

- *Note*: There are certain exceptions to personal liability for decisions made by managers in furtherance of their business obligations. That is, a doctrine known as the "business judgment rule" protects high-level managers from liability to shareholders for decisions that ultimately harm the corporation and its shareholders. This doctrine is a common defense when shareholders sue directors and officers.

What are the ways that a business entity can lose its liability shield?

A business entity offering personal liability protection may forfeit that protection if the Secretary of State's office or the court disregards the business entity. As previously stated, the Secretary of State may dissolve a business entity for failing to follow entity maintenance requirements. More commonly, a plaintiff who is suing the business may attack the business entity status (i.e., attempt to pierce the corporate veil). If the court disregards the business entity status, the owner(s) of the business will be personally liable for any debts or tortious conduct by the business or its employees.

- *Note*: A plaintiff who is suing a business may realize that the business has insufficient funds to satisfy a judgment against the business. While the business may lack sufficient assets, the owners of the business may have extensive assets. In such a case, a plaintiff may seek to attack the business entity status to subject the owner of the business entity to personal liability for the tortious conduct of the business.

How can a business owner do more to protect herself from personal liability?

The first step is to follow all of the business maintenance requirements. This is necessary to maintain any level of protection. This is not a complete solution, as all of the business entities have varying degrees of potential personal liability for owners of the business. The degree of potential liability varies with the title and position held within the business. For example, a director of a corporation may have less exposure to liability than a member in a LLC by virtue of her role in the venture. Specifically defining the role and authority of each owner of the business can help to avoid personal liability in many scenarios. Further, outlining procedures for employer conduct and conducting training on issues of liability can help avoid legal disputes. We devote considerable time below exploring the potential liability of an individual carrying on business as each type of business entity.

- *Note*: A good way to protect one's self from your own tortious conduct is by purchasing liability insurance. This may protect the business as well as the business owners.

TAXATION OF BUSINESS ENTITIES

Taxation of the applicable business entity is a primary consideration when choosing an entity form under which to operate. Taxation of business entities, however, is a very complicated topic. We give an overview of business taxation in a separate chapter.

CHAPTER 3: AGENCY LAW & LIABILITY

What is agency law and why is it important in understanding business entities?

Agency law regards the rules governing the rights and obligations of an individual or business acting on behalf of another individual or business. Using the vocabulary of agency law, the agent acts on behalf of the principal. The agent interacts with third-parties. Having knowledge of basic agency law is important in understanding the control and authority available to individuals involved in the business. Further, agency law governs the liability of the business, business owners, and the agents.

Who is a principal?

In the context of business law, the principal is generally the one soliciting or responsible for the activities of the agent. Restated, the principal employs an agent to act on her behalf.

Who is an agent?

Agents have authority to act on behalf of the principal. Principals hire agents to do tasks and represent them in transactions. All employees are agents of the employer. However, in some cases, someone who is not an employee can be an agent.

- *Example*: Eric hires Tom to deliver packages for his retail business. Eric is an employee and is the agent of Tom's business. He represents the business in delivering packages, receiving money, and any other responsibilities in the scope of his work.

What is an independent contractor and how does it relate to agency law?

An independent contractor is generally not an agent. The reason is because a business does not directly control an independent contractor. Legally, an independent contractor operates her own business and provides services to any other business on a contract basis. An employee, on the other hand, does not have her own business. She carries out tasks on behalf of and under the control of a business.

- *Example*: Tom approaches Jim's Garage, LLC and offers to cut the grass for $20. Tom is an independent contractor because the relationship does not involve work within the ordinary course of operations, nor does it entail a great deal of direct control. However, Tom may simply ask Jim if he needs any help with any mechanic work. If Jim's Garage takes him on, the relationship begins to look more like an employer-employee relationship as Jim actively controls Jim's activity throughout the day and the activity is in the ordinary course of operations.

How can a non-employee (such as an independent contractor) be an agent of the principal?

Agency status generally arises by virtue of the amount of authority granted to an individual.

Thus, an agency relationship arises when someone, who may or may not be an employee (such as an independent contractor), is granted sufficient authority to undertake action on behalf of the principal.

- *Note:* A professional services provider (such as an accountant or attorney) could be a non-employee agent of the principal.

Who is a third party and why is the concept important?

The agent interacts with a third party on behalf of the principal. A common purpose of the agent is to create a binding contract or relationship between the principal and the third party.

- *Note*: This can be an employee-agent purchasing goods or soliciting sales on behalf of the employer-principal.

What special duties does the agent owe to the principal?

The agent, in acting on behalf of the principal, has the following duties:

- To act for the principal's advantage and not to act to benefit the agent at the principal's expense (a "duty of loyalty"),
- To keep the principal fully informed,
- To obey instructions, and
- To account to the principal for monies handled.

Each state's common law establishes the above-referenced duties. While this list is not exclusive, it does identify the major duties owed by the agent to the principal.

What is vicarious liability?

Vicarious liability is when an individual or business is contractually or civilly liable for the actions of another individual or business. Vicarious liability is an element of agency law. An agent may have authority to bind the principal in contract. Likewise, the actions of the agent may subject the principal to vicarious liability.

- *Note*: In the context of business entities, it would be where the owner or business entity is liable for the activity of its members or employees (i.e., the agents of the business). This liability could be under contract (debts, duties, etc.) or tort (negligence, intentional conduct, strict liability) law.

What is respondeat superior?

Respondeat superior is a specific type of vicarious liability. It specifically regards the situation where an employer is liable for the tortious actions of an agent-employee. The employer's liability turns on whether the agent is under the control of the employer when committing the tortious conduct. As discussed above, an employer-employee relationship is characterized by control that exceeds that of the independent contractor. As such, an employer will be liable for the conduct of the employee which the employer actively controls. Control is commonly determined by looking at whether the employee was acting in furtherance of the principal's business.

- *Example*: Samantha, an employee, is delivering packages for her employer's business. She has a traffic accident with another vehicle and it is her fault. The other individual is hurt and sues the employee and the employer business. The employer business will be liable for the employee's negligent activity because it was done in furtherance of the principal or employer's business activity. Another way of saying that it was done in furtherance of the employer's business activity is that it was within the scope of employment.

When is an employer-principal not liable for the actions of the employee-agent?

As stated above, the employee must be under the control of the employer. Control is commonly determined by looking at whether the employee was acting in furtherance of the principal's business. If the employee was acting "within the scope of her employment", her actions may subject the principal to civil liability. An employee who substantially deviates from the purpose or scope of her employment is deemed to act on her own behalf. This is known as a 'frolic-and-detour' from the scope of employment.

- *Example*: In the above scenario, suppose the employee delivers the packages and completes her job responsibilities. She then travels in the employer's truck to a friend's house. The employer has specific rules in place against using the business vehicle for personal reasons. All of the employees know these rules. The traffic accident occurs when the employee is backing out of the friend's driveway. This is likely a sufficient frolic and detour from the employee's responsibilities to relieve the employer from vicarious liability for her actions.

What can an employer recover from an employee for acts that make the employer vicariously liable?

An employer who must pay for an employee's tortious conduct under *respondeat superior* may legally sue the employee for reimbursement.

- *Note*: In reality, this rarely happens, as the employee often lacks sufficient resources to satisfy such a judgment. Misconduct by a corporate executive is an example of a situation where a business may sue or seek reimbursement for damages paid for an executive's tortious conduct.

When is an employer contractually liable for an agent's Acts?

There are three primary types of agent authority (actual, implied, and apparent) that are sufficient to establish liability between a principal and third party.

- *Note*: Each type of authority has the ability to bind the employer in contract. The extent of this ability varies with the employee, task, third-party, etc.

What is actual authority?

Actual authority is the express authority granted by the principal to the agent. Express authority can be written, verbal, or inferred by the conduct of the principal and agent. Written authority would be a provision of an employment contract or other written document directing the agent's activity. Verbal authority would be a direct order or request for the agent to undertake a certain activity. Authority inferred from conduct is where the principal, through his or her conduct, signals to the agent that she has a given level of authority to take action.

- *Note*: The key determinant for when an agent has actual authority is whether the principal intends a certain level of authority. In some cases, an agent may have actual authority from the principal to undertake an activity and not know it.

What is implied authority?

Implied authority, as the name indicates, is implied from the context of a situation or when interacting with third parties. Implied authority is perceived by third-parties interacting with the agent. Authority may be implied by a position title or from a past course of conduct with the third party.

- *Example*: Julie works for Alice. Julie's title is vice president of operations and she regularly interacts with a third-party supply, Supply Co. Julie purchases business equipment from Supply Co for the business for which she did not have actual authority. Alice does not want to pay and accept the equipment from the Supply Co under the grounds that Julie did not have authority to make the purchase. In such a situation, Supply Co would be able to show Julie had implied authority under two principals. First, Julie's title implies that she has authority to purchase equipment. Second, Julie's past course of dealing with Supply Co indicates that she had the ability to make purchases.

What is apparent authority?

Apparent authority regards a representation of authority by the agent that is reasonable to the third-party. This determination turns on the nature of the representation and the context of the situation. Generally, it requires that the third-party rely on the representation to her detriment. If the third party does so, a court may impute the represented level of authority to the agent. The business will be bound by the actions of the agent. The theory is that an employer stands in the best position to limit its agent's activity and should bear the risk that she will step outside of her authority.

- *Example*: Alex tells John Car Dealer that he has authority to purchase a new vehicle on behalf of Tom's business. Alex is Tom's employee. John knows that Alex frequently enters into business contracts on behalf of Tom's business. John has never dealt with Alex personally. In this context, it may be reasonable to believe that Alex has this authority. If

John Car Dealer will suffer a significant detriment if Tom returns the truck on the grounds that Alex did not have authority to purchase it, then there may be sufficient apparent authority for John Car Dealer to enforce the contract.

- *Note*: The principal can avoid liability for the apparent authority of agents by making third parties aware of the limited authority of the agent. If the principal does so, she will not be bound by the actions of that agent that exceed the stated authority. It would be unreasonable for the third party to rely on the representations of authority by the agent that exceed the authority indicated to the third party by the principal.

What is ratification?

Ratification concerns a situation where an agent acts beyond her authority. If the principal then accepts the actions taken by the agent, then she has ratified the activity and is bound or liable for the actions. Ratification can occur through words or conduct of the principal.

- *Note*: If a principal ratifies the unauthorized activity with a third party, this could give rise to apparent authority in later transactions. If the principal has ever ratified a transaction, she should take care to notify third parties of the limited scope of the transaction and authority of the agent.

CHAPTER 4: TAXATION OF THE OWNER AND BUSINESS ENTITY

What do I need to know about business taxation to effectively understand business entities?

Within this text we review the basics of how each business entity and its owners are taxed on its profits. We explain the issues surrounding the distribution and retention of proceeds by the entity. Further, we review the basic rules surrounding active and passive losses and the ability to carry losses forward and backwards to offset profits. Understanding basic taxation concepts as they apply to each entity type will give you sufficient background to understand the important tax considerations in a transaction by a given business entity.

How are individuals taxed on their personal incomes?

Individuals pay a percentage of their adjusted gross income (AGI) in Federal and State income tax. AGI is calculated as an individual's gross income, minus all deductions (either the standard deduction or itemized deductions) and the individual's personal exemption. The standard deduction in 2014 is $6,200. The personal exemption is $3,950. A person's gross income is comprised of wages or other income, dividends, and investment interest, gains, dividends, rents, royalties, etc.

Wages or other income consists of any money earned as an employee or through one's own business activity. A business activity could be the provision of any form of goods or services to another person. Long-term capital gains (gains on certain assets held longer than 12 months) and dividends are taxed at different rates than other forms of gross income. Short-term capital gains are taxed at ordinary income rates.

The income tax rates for wages and other income are tiered. All individuals pay a fixed percentage on the first several thousand dollars of their AGI, a fixed percentage on the next several thousand, etc.

- *Example*: The 2014 tax brackets are 10, 15, 25, 28, 33, 35, and 39.6%. The dollar amount of income that fits in each bracket depends upon whether the individual files as a single taxpayer, married filing separately, head of household, or married filing jointly.

The tax rate for long-term capital gains and qualified dividends may also be tiered based upon income. While they are included in gross income, qualified dividends and long-term capital gains are subject to different tax rates from other sources of income.

- *Example*: In 2014 long-term capital gains and qualified dividends are taxed at 0, 15, and 20%. The 0% rate applies to individuals in the 10% and 15% income tax brackets. The 15% rate applies to individuals in the 20, 28, 33 and 35% income tax brackets. The 20% rate applies to individuals in the 39% income tax bracket.

Staying aware of 1) the tax rates for corporations and individuals and 2) the types of income is important when determining the most favorable tax situation for a business activity. Keep in mind that the applicable tax brackets and percentages change often.

- *Note*: Visit www.IRS.gov for the current applicable tax rates and income levels.

How are business entities taxed?

Business entities are either not taxed at all, or they are taxed at a corporate rate. If a business entity is classified as a pass-through tax entity, then it does not pay income taxes. Rather, the business owners pay taxes on any business profits. Restated, the profits or losses from the business activity pass through to the individual and are reported on her individual income tax form.

- *Note*: Individual taxpayers report pass-through business income on their personal tax returns.

Businesses that pay taxes (corporations or businesses that choose to be taxed as corporations) are taxed at the corporate rate. Like the individual tax system, the corporate tax rate is tiered.

- *Example*: In 2014 the applicable corporate tax rates are 10, 25, 34, 39, 34, 35, 38, and 35%, depending upon the amount of taxable corporate income.

Corporations (and entities that choose to be taxed as corporations) are subject to double taxation. That is, the corporation pays income taxes on profit as explained above. Any distributions of corporate income to shareholders is taxed to the shareholder at the applicable dividend rate. The shareholder reports those dividends on her personal income tax form.

- *Note*: Startup owners who chose corporate tax status attempt to balance the payment of wages and dividends to affect the lowest tax rate possible. Depending upon the individual's tax rate, the corporate tax rate, and the duty to pay other taxes (e.g., Social Security, Medicare, FUTA, SUTA), there may be a way to pay less taxes *via* the corporate tax regime than *via* pass-through taxation.

What are payroll and self-employment taxes?

Payroll and self-employment taxes are made up of Social Security and Medicare taxes. These taxes were authorized under the Federal Insurance Contribution Act (FICA). Payroll taxes are the taxes withheld from an employee's payroll. The employer matches these funds and deposits them with the Internal Revenue Service (IRS). A self-employed individual is the employer and employee. As such, she has to pay both portions of the payroll tax.

- *Note*: Some types of business entities allow business owners to receive a percentage of business profits as passive investors and not pay self-employment taxes. These taxes are generally assessed against individuals who provide services to the business. This becomes tricky as some business entities allow the investor to take part in the business activity, which, even though they are passive investors, may take their earnings subject to self-employment taxes.

What other special rules apply to how businesses are taxed?

The Internal Revenue Code (IRC) is extremely complex. Two important issues concerning how individuals and businesses are taxed are the reporting of profits or losses and the individual's basis in her business interest. These rules affect the amount of taxable income or loss attributable to the business and the individual in a number of ways.

- *Note*: Startups are very concerned with the ability to defer profits, reinvest in the business, and achieve maximum gains. These objectives make the use of losses to offset income and the entrepreneur or investor's basis in the business particularly relevant.

What happens if the business has losses?

Startups are particularly prone to have considerable losses. These businesses seek to grow rapidly by employing available debt and investor capital and reinvesting all profits back into the business. This rapid growth often creates large loss accumulations. Corporations (or entities that are taxed as corporations) maintain losses within the business entity. These losses are used to offset business income. Generally, losses may be carried back for 2 years and forward for 20 years.

Business entities with pass-through taxation do not retain losses within the business entity. Losses are passed through to owners based either on the percentage of ownership or pursuant to a special allocation in a partnership. The losses can generally be used to offset the individual's profits. There are, however, limitations on the ability of individuals to use or employ these losses. The most important limitations regard basis, at-risk limitations, and active and passive loss rules. Losses must clear all three of these hurdles to be used by owners. Each of these limitations is discussed below.

- *Note:* The use of losses is a significant concern for equity investors. Part of the value that investors attribute to a startup at the time of investment takes into consideration the ability to use these losses to offset income from other investments.

What is basis?

"Basis" is largely a tax concept. By definition, basis is the value that an individual pays for an asset. If the asset is later sold or disposed of for a higher amount, there is a gain. If it is sold for a lower amount, there is a loss. One unique aspect of basis in a business entity is that it includes the value paid for the equity ownership, as well as the value of any business liabilities assumed in a partnership or LLC.

- *Example*: ReadyBiz, LLC purchases equipment for $10,000 in cash and signs a promissory note for $15,000, ReadyBiz's basis in the equipment is $25,000. If ReadBiz purchases multiple pieces of equipment together, then the tax basis must be attributed to the item based on its individual value. Determining the basis is important in determining tax consequence when the equipment is later sold.

33

A business owner's basis increases as more funds are invested in the business. In an entity that elects pass-through taxation, the owner's basis further increases if the business makes a profit that is taxed to owners but not distributed. Conversely, if the business suffers a loss that is deducted on the equity holder's personal tax return, then it reduces the basis in the business.

- *Example*: Sam starts a new business named Store, Inc., and elects to be taxed as a pass-through entity under Subsection S of the IRC. She then invests $10,000 in the business. Her basis in the business is therefore $10,000. In the first year, the business makes a profit of $5,000. Since profits pass through to the owners, Sam pays personal income taxes on this $5,000, but leaves it in the business (i.e., reinvests it). Sam's basis in the business is now $ 15,000. The following year, the business loses $3,000. Same reports these losses on his personal income tax return. His basis in the business is reduced to $12,000 because he used the $3,000 loses to offset other income.

- *Example*: In the above example, Sam may elect for Store, Inc. to be subject to corporate taxation under Subsection C of the IRC. In such a case, Sam will only pay dividend taxes on distributions of profits by Store, Inc., to her. If she pays tax on those distributions, then reinvests them back in the business, her basis in the business increases.

- *Note*: A person's basis cannot be reduced below zero ($0). If this happens, the person will be assessed a tax to bring the basis back up to zero.

The depreciation of assets reduces the basis of those assets because it allows for the return of value paid for the asset in the form of depreciation deductions. The reduced basis is known as the adjusted basis. Entrepreneurs and equity investors track their basis to determine any gain or potential income tax liabilities from future distribution of profits or sale of the business.

- *Example*: Store, Inc., claims $500 of depreciation deductions on its equipment. The adjusted basis would be $9,500 (i.e., take the $10,000 basis from the above purchase of equipment and subtract $500). Depreciation, amortization, and deducted losses are effects that can lower a business' basis in equipment.

What are the basis and at-risk limitations?

An equity holder's basis is generally determined by a combination of the amount of an owner's investment (capital basis), and, for pass-through tax entities, the amount that the investor has at-risk in the business venture (debt basis). As the name implies, at-risk means that the equity investor has the possibility of losing these funds. An equity investor who invests funds in the business venture in exchange for equity ownership has an at-risk basis of that amount. In some pass-through entities (excluding an S corporation), an equity holder's at-risk amount also includes any loans to the business that the equity holder personally guarantees.

- *Example*: Victoria invests $1,000 in John's business (an LLC). Victoria also personally guarantees a SBA loan to the business for $500. Her basis in the business is $1,500

($1,000 + $500).

- *Note*: Basis is essentially the outer limit of what you may be able to deduct. At-risk elements may prevent full recognition of loss to the extent a partner is not subject to risk of repayment of some or all of the partnership debt allocated to her.

The ability to raise one's basis and at-risk amount in a business by personally guaranteeing a loan is a strong consideration in choosing an entity form. Business owners may need to use business losses to offset other income. Basis may limit an owner's ability to use those loses, as she cannot deduct losses that reduce her basis below zero ($0).

- *Example*: In the example above, Victoria's basis is $1,500. The LLC takes a loss in a year for which Victoria's allocation is $2,000. She has other income of more than $2,000 that she would like to offset with the LLC losses. Unfortunately, Victoria is limited by her basis amount and may only offset $1,500 of her other income (assuming other rules of offset are met). If she offsets $1,500 of her other income with the LLC losses, her basis in the business will be reduced to $0. Likewise, her at-risk amount is now zero.

- *Note*: The ability to use loans made to the business to raise an owner's basis is a complicated subject. In general, the ability to include a guaranteed loan amount in basis turns on what kind of entity the business is and on whether the owner-guarantor has recourse against anyone (including the business entity or other owners) if the business fails to repay the loan. Often, if the business owner bears all of the risk for the business' loan default, without the ability to seek contribution or reimbursement from others, then the guaranteed loan amount may be included in one's basis.

What is a passive loss?

Business profits and losses in pass-through tax entities are divided into active profits or losses and passive profits or losses for tax purposes. Active losses are business losses incurred in a business in which the equity holder is an active participant in the business activity. The rules for determining active participation are numerous, but they are mostly based on the number of hours and percentage of time spent working in the business. Therefore, any losses that pass through to an investor who is not an active participant in the business are considered passive losses. Classification of losses affects the ability to offset other profits (profits from other activities not related to the business) that the investor includes in her personal income. Passive losses can be used to offset passive income; likewise, active losses can be used to offset active income. Active income includes wages, income from substantial involvement in a pass-through business entity, along with several other sources. Unused active losses can generally be carried backward for two years and forward for twenty years to offset active income. Unused passive losses are carried forward as such to offset passive income. The losses can also be claimed to offset gains at the time of sale of the equity interest.

- *Example*: Tina is a passive investor in a partnership. In a given year she earns $3,000 as her share of partnership profits. At the same time, Tina is a passive investor in an S corporation that loses $2,500 that year. She also owns an interest in and is actively involved in the operations of an LLC. The LLC loses $500 that given year that is allocated to Tina. In this scenario, Tina can offset the $3,000 passive income with the $2,500 passive loss. This leaves $500 of passive income that is taxable. The $500 in losses from her LLC interest is active in nature. She cannot use these active losses to offset the passive income. The active losses can, however, be carried forward to offset future active income.

- *Note*: Passive income is subject to ordinary income tax, but is exempt from self-employment taxes in partnerships. Uncertainty exists over the taxation of LLC income for seemingly passive investors. That is, regarding LLCs that are taxed as pass-through entities, the IRS has taken the stance that any distributions to an LLC member is subject to self-employment tax. This is a notable difference between the two entity forms. The IRS has proposed regulations to change this disparity.

How does the IRS determine what is passive and active income or losses?

The determination of whether income is active or passive is based upon whether the individual materially participates in the venture. There are several considerations that go into the material participation test. A person materially participates in an activity if:

- She participates for more than 500 hours in business activities,
- Her activity constitutes all of the business activity in the tax year,
- She participates 100 hours and her activity is as much as any other business member,
- She participates in all significant participation activities for more than 500 hours per year,
- She materially participates in the business during any 5 of the past 10 years (3 years if a personal service business), or
- She participates on a regular, continuous, and substantial way during the past year.

- *Note*: This issue arises in the context of partnership-taxed entities and S corporations.

What happens if the business does not distribute any of the profits to the owners?

A corporation or an entity being taxed as a corporation distributes profits to its shareholders as dividends. If the corporation determines that it will not issue a dividend, then the corporation pays taxes on the profits at its corporate tax rate and that is all. The money is retained as retained earnings and is available for use in the business. If the business is a pass-through entity, there is no taxation at the business entity level. The share of profits allocable to the equity holder (based upon her share of ownership or based upon any special allocation in a partnership) will be reported on her personal income tax statement. If the business retains the profits and does not actually distribute the funds, the equity holder will still have to pay taxes on the funds. This is known as creating "phantom income", as the equity holder may have to pay taxes on income she did not actually receive.

- *Example:* Audrey is a 50% owner of an LLC with Eddie. At the end of the year the LLC makes a profit of $10,000. Both parties determine that it is best to not withdraw any funds from the LLC and to reinvest the profits in growing the business. The LLC is a pass-through tax entity. Both Audrey and Eddie will have to pay taxes on $5,000 at their ordinary individual income tax rates, even though they did not take any money out of the business. Once they pay the taxes on the profit, however, each owner's basis will be increased by $5,000. This may reduce that tax burden at a later sale of the owner's equity. Further, they will not have to pay tax again when the profits are actually distributed to them.

- *Note:* Most startups avoid this issue by reinvesting all profits into operations during the tax year and not reporting a profit in that year.

Another common situation giving rise to phantom income arises during the initial capitalization of the business. When a member of a business entity receives an equity interest in the business in exchange for work or services performed to the business, the individual is taxed on the value of that equity interest at their ordinary individual income tax rates. The amount of tax is based upon the value of the equity interest as measured by the existing assets in the business. The individual receives a valuable asset (equity interest), but doesn't receive actual cash. Often the equity interest received is illiquid, which creates a difficult situation for the new equity holder. Nonetheless, the equity holder will pay taxes on the value of equity received with little or no ability to liquidate that interest to pay the assessed taxes.

- *Example:* Eric and Tom form an LLC. Eric invests $1,000 in the business, and Tom provides labor. They divide ownership interest in the business equally. At the end of the year, the business breaks even. Tom will be taxed on the equity interest that he received as a result of his labor. Since the business was worth the value of its assets ($1,000) at the time that Tom received an interest in the business, he will be taxed as if he received $500 for his labor.

CHAPTER 5: THE SOLE PROPRIETORSHIP

In this chapter we explore the sole proprietorship and its characteristics as a business entity. Many people do not think of or recognize the sole proprietorship as a form of business entity. This is primarily because the boundary between the individual entrepreneur and business entity is often blurred. This chapter should supply you with sufficient information to understand where the boundary exists in a given business.

How are sole proprietorships created?

To create a sole proprietorship the individual entrepreneur simply has to carry on some activity with the intention of seeking a profit. It is really that simple. It arises when a single individual carries on an activity for a profit (or loss). No formal filing or documentation is required.

- *Example*: Suppose that Jake is walking down the street and see a man in his lawn raking leaves. The man asks Jake if he would like to earn some money by raking up the rest of the leaves. The man says that he will pay Jake $30. In this situation, Jake is undertaking an activity with the intent of making a profit. Jake is not an employee of anyone else; rather, he is undertaking the work as a service provider. This means that he is a default sole proprietor.

- *Note*: By definition, a sole proprietorship involves one person. The business entity cannot contain more than one owner.

The definition of a sole proprietorship has two primary components: 1) an activity, and 2) intent to earn a profit. This definition is very broad and covers a broad range of activities. For example, the activity could be as little as making a phone call to put resources in order. This could make a person's actions or activity into an unintended business entity. The important thing to remember is that the entrepreneur does not have to intend to start a business and the type or manner of activity that she undertakes is irrelevant.

The second requirement is that one intend to earn a profit. This definition can be somewhat misleading, as not every sole proprietorship makes a profit. This requirement is interpreted to mean any sort of activity that intends to generate revenue. Most businesses lose money early in their lives. Undertaking an activity with the intent of ultimately generating a profit is sufficient to satisfy this requirement.

- *Example*: Tom starts a business and seeks revenue from outside investors. He expresses his intent to reinvest every penny of profit toward growth. Tom knows that he will likely suffer a loss every year early on in an attempt to grow the business's volume and revenue. He believes that at some later point in time he will be able to cut expenses and produce a profit or sell the business at a high valuation based upon its revenue. Even though Tom realizes that he will not earn a profit in the immediate future, he is still a sole proprietor. The same is true for charitable undertakings that produce revenue.

- *Note*: Numerous other requirements may exist for the sole proprietor. For example, she will likely have to obtain a business license from the local government before undertaking business. She will have to do a fictitious name filing if she operates under a name other than her own name. Further, she will need to set up an employer identification number (EIN) if she plans to have employees for her business.

Who has ownership and control over a sole proprietorship?

The sole proprietor exercises complete control and is the sole owner of the business. As the name implies, a sole proprietorship can only have one owner. Adding another member to the sole proprietorship changes the entity form.

- *Note*: A sole proprietorship can have employees who work in the business. The key to this relationship is that the employees cannot earn ownership interest in the business activity. This will preclude any profit sharing arrangements between the owner and employee. The owner should be careful when compensating an employee based upon the amount of revenue produced. Such compensation should be carefully structured as a bonus system on a base salary.

What is the continuity of a sole proprietorship?

If the entrepreneur stops carrying on the business activity, the sole proprietorship ceases to exist. Ownership in the sole proprietorship cannot be transferred because the business activity is unique to the individual. The name, property, activity can be transferred, but the actual organizational identity is unique to the individual carrying on the business. The business entity will exist as long as the sole proprietor wishes to continue doing business.

- *Example*: Tom, a sole proprietor, decides to pass his business down to his son, Jerry. Tom can pass to Jerry the name of the business, the equipment, any intellectual property, etc.; but, he cannot pass the actual business. Jerry will take the assets and start his own sole proprietorship. This is important as any contractual relationships that exist cannot be transferred. Jerry will have to re-establish those relationships when he takes over and begins his sole proprietorship.

- *Note*: Business activities are often passed from owner to owner. This is done by transferring the actual assets of the business. For tax purposes this re-establishes a basis in the assets and begins the business activity anew. All business relationships will generally have to be re-established (such as the establishment of bank accounts, the supplier relationship, etc.).

What is the personal liability of the sole proprietor?

The sole proprietor lacks the personal liability protection provided by several other business entity types. The main disadvantage of carrying on business as a sole proprietorship is that the owner is personally liable for any contract obligations or torts committed as part of the business activity. An individual is generally liable in tort for her own actions; however, she is also personally liable for the torts of any employees committed in the course of business operations. This fact exposes the sole proprietor to a great deal of risk.

- *Example:* Jack starts a business providing cleaning services to local businesses. His business is successful and he immediately hires several workers. One day a worker accidentally hits a customer in the eye with a broom when he is sweeping the store. Recall from Chapter 3 that an employee is an agent of the business. The customer is injured and sues Jack's business. Jack will be personally liable for any judgment against the business. This means that his personal assets (e.g., home, car, bank account) will be at risk in a lawsuit.

- *Note*: A sole proprietor's potential personal liability for the torts of the business's employees begs the question, who are employees of the business? Recall, this question concerns the amount of control the business owner exercises over the individual. If the business owner exercises strong controls over the individual, then she is likely an employee. If the individual more closely resembles a separate business hired by the business owner for a specific task, then she is likely an independent contractor rather than an employee.

How is the sole proprietorship taxed?

In general, tax reporting for the sole proprietorship is relatively simple when compared to other business entity types. Individuals report their personal income tax liability on Form 1040 (or some variation thereof). The sole proprietor does not have to prepare or file a separate tax return for the business entity. The Form 1040 allows the individual to report any income from business operations on their personal income tax return on Schedule C.

- *Example*: Melanie has a 9-5 job at a large company. She will receive a W-2 at the end of the year indicating her wages received. She is also a sole proprietor in that she earns money providing professional services to clients. This line of work is not related to her 9-5 job. She will report the W-2 wages on line 1 of the IRS Form 1040. She will report the income and expenses from her business activity on Schedule C of her 1040.

- *Note*: Like any business, the sole proprietor will report all revenue generated by the business and all expenses of operations. She must also keep track of specific issues, such as depreciation schedules on business equipment. Despite the simplicity of tax reporting for sole proprietorship income, there are several other tax considerations for the sole proprietor.

What are the sole proprietor's other tax reporting obligations?

Understanding the tax reporting obligations of the sole proprietor requires an understanding of the general tax withholding and reporting system. Most notably among these obligations are the requirement to withhold and report sales and use taxes and self-employment taxes.

- *Note*: A sole proprietorship, like other business entities, has to withhold taxes for its owner and employees. Further, it has to withhold any special business taxes imposed by the state or locality. The withheld taxes must be transferred to the appropriate government agency on the appropriate schedule.

How does sales and use tax withholding work?

Businesses that sell any sort of good are subject to sales and use tax. Sales tax is the amount that the merchant must charge to customers who purchase the good. Sales tax is generally a fixed percentage of the value of the good. Other taxes that accompany sales tax may also apply for specialty occupations, such as merchants selling luxury goods, hotels, and restaurants. The merchant must collect the tax from the customer and not simply pay the taxes from the proceeds of the sale. The taxes withheld must be deposited with the state's department of revenue on a regular basis.

- *Example*: Jason sells custom furniture that he manufactures in his wood shop. The chairs retail for $300 each. The state sales tax on goods of this kind is 7%. When a customer purchases a chair, Jason must charge the customer $321 ($300 + $21) at the time of purchase.

- *Note*: The taxing state is the location where the good was sold. It does not matter the location where the seller is located. Many states allow that, if the customer is located out of state and Jason ships the item to him, then Jason does not have to collect sales tax.

Use tax is a separate tax that applies to the purchase of goods. Specifically, use taxes are assessed against goods purchased for resale. Use tax is assessed when goods are purchased in another state at a lower sales tax rate. The merchant must pay the tax rate difference to the state where the good is sold.

- *Example*: You purchase a widget from state A. The applicable sales tax is 5%. You then resell that widget in state B. The applicable sales tax in state B is 6%. You will owe use tax to state B in the amount of 1% of the value of the widget.

- *Note*: The reason that the seller must pay the tax rate difference to the state where the good is sold is because that is the state to which income tax is owed. Even if the good was intended for sale in one state, if it may be sold in another. Therefore, the use tax will become due in the state in which the good is sold.

What are the employee and self-employment tax withholding rules?

Sales and use tax is not the sole proprietor's only tax withholding obligation. She also is charged with withholding income taxes from an employee's wages. The employee must fill out form W-4 to provide necessary withholding information, which is then used to determine the amount of income to withhold. The withheld wages serve to satisfy the employee's federal and state income tax obligations. The employer will also withhold Federal Unemployment Tax (FUTA), State Unemployment tax (SUTA), Social Security and Medicare taxes (known as Federal

Insurance Contributions Act or FICA taxes) from the employee's wages. The employer also has the obligations to match the employee's FICA taxes with business funds. She deposits all of the taxes withheld at regular intervals with the IRS or state taxing authority.

- *Example*: William has a lawn care business. In the last year he has expanded to hire four employees. William will have to withhold estimated income taxes from the employees' paychecks and deposit them with the IRS and state department of revenue. William must also withhold FICA taxes from each employee's paycheck. William will match these amounts and then deposit them with the IRS.

- *Note*: The Social Security portion of the FICA taxes is capped at a certain amount for the individual. The Medicare portion of the taxes has no cap and is assessed against the total wages of the employee.

The sole proprietor is subject to a unique situation with regard to tax withholding. The sole proprietor is, in effect, her own employee. She must pay income taxes and self-employment taxes on any income earned from the sole proprietorship. Self-employment taxes are made up of a combination of the employer and employee's Social Security and Medicare tax obligations. She will deposit this amount regularly with the taxing authorities. She must also deposit funds to cover any expected income tax obligations. Failure to deposit sufficient funds to cover the sole proprietor's income tax obligations may result in a penalty.

- *Example*: Tori is a cosmetologist, specializing in hair coloring. She has her own hair practice that she runs out of her home. As a sole proprietor, she will have to make estimated tax payments to the IRS and state department of revenue to cover her income tax liability. Further, she will have to withhold self-employment taxes and deposit those taxes with the IRS.

- *Note*: The fact that a sole proprietor pays twice the amount of Social Security and Medicare taxes as an employee leads owners and investors in businesses to seek alternative business entities to shield themselves from most or all of the self-employment tax obligation.

CHAPTER 6: GENERAL PARTNERSHIPS & JOINT VENTURES

GENERAL PARTNERSHIP (GP)

What is a GP?

A GP is an agreement between two or more persons to share a common interest in a commercial endeavor and to share its profits and losses. This definition contains similar elements to the sole proprietorship, but requires more than one person.

- *Note*: It is important to understand that a GP is a default entity. That is, the partners do not have to intend to create a GP, nor do they have to realize that a GP has been formed. The GP arises pursuant to the activity of the partners.

What is a GP agreement and why is it important?

A partnership agreement is the governing document for any type of partnership. Partnership agreements are not mandatory, but it is advisable for any partnership to have an agreement governing the partnership relationship. In the absence of a formal agreement, states have default rules governing the operations of the partnership and the relationship between the partners. While the default rules are comprehensive, they often do not always align with the specific intent of the parties.

- *Note:* Most states have adopted the Uniform Partnership Act as the rules governing partnerships. Some states, however, have unique common law rules (such as rules affecting the duties between partners) that apply to the partnership relationship.

What are the important provisions to cover in a partnership agreement?

A partnership agreement, like other business entity governance documents, should be drafted to address the specific concerns of the business and the partners. Below are some of the major considerations to address within any partnership agreement.

- <u>Partnership Name</u>: Make certain that you check the availability of the name with the Secretary of State's office. Further, if you are going to operate under a name other than that of the partners, you should make a fictitious name filing or "doing-business-as" filing with the Secretary of State or local authorities.

- <u>Ownership Interest</u>: What will the allocation of ownership interest be? What will be each partner's contribution to the partnership in exchange for her share of partnership interest?

- <u>Entitlements of Partners</u>: The default rule for partnerships is that each partner is entitled to an equal portion of profits and losses of the business. If the parties wish for an alternative allocation of ownership or entitlements, then the partnership agreement should address the allocation. One unique aspect about a partnership is that, with certain exceptions, partnerships can allocate profits and losses in a different percentage than the ownership structure. Further, the agreement should address the timing and amount of any distribution of partnership profits or assets. This is an extremely important provision, as the partners may have varying ideas regarding when and how much they are able to draw from partnership profits.

- <u>Authority of Partners</u>: Who will have decision-making authority within the partnership? Will one party have authority over certain decisions? Will certain decisions require consensus? Which partners have authority to bind the business in contract? Authority is important, as the default rules provide each partner the authority to act on behalf of the business and bind the partnership (and all partners) in contract.

- <u>Management Responsibilities</u>: It may be a good idea to designate primary responsibilities to certain partners. Often partners have conflicting ideas over who should be in charge of which business activities. While these provisions do not have to be concrete, they provide some guidance as to the responsibilities of each partner.

- <u>Addition of New Partners</u>: What is the process of bringing on new partners? What is the required consent from the parties? Does it require unanimous consent or simply a majority? How is the allocation of any new partnership interest determined?

- <u>Continuity of the Partnership</u>: What happens if a partner dissociates or is expelled? What is the procedure for the partner leaving or exiting? How is the partner's interest handled? Does the partnership continue on or must the business be wound up? Is the result different if the dissociation is not voluntary? What if a partner passes away? Who bears responsibility in any of these situations?

- <u>Partnership Disputes</u>: How will partnership disputes be resolved? Will there be a formal process for mediating disputes? Will the partners use a third-party arbitrator? If so, what are the rules surrounding it?

How is the GP formed?

As previously stated, the GP arises by default pursuant to the conduct of the parties. The partners do not have to call themselves partners or even see themselves as being in a GP. The GP arises pursuant to their activity. They simply have to carry on an activity in concert with the intent of sharing profits or losses.

- *Example*: Dave begins scouring the neighborhood for metal items that people leave on the curb as trash to be collected by the garbage man. Dave knows that he can take the metal to a scrapyard and make some money. He asks Laura if she will take his truck and cruise her neighborhood for metal. He says that he will give her 40% of the value of any metal collected. In this case Dave has agreed to share ownership in the business and Laura will be a partner. If Dave had said he would pay her $7.50 per hour and give her 20% of the value of any metal she collects, then Dave would still be a sole proprietor.

- *Note*: Documenting the relationship between individuals in a business activity can serve to characterize the relationship as a GP or employer-employee relationship. If you wish to hire an individual (not bring her on as a partner) and compensate her with a share of the profits, then you will need to document the employment relationship. This may require special structuring of any profit sharing as a bonus paid to the employee, rather than as an ownership percentage in any profits.

What other steps should I follow in forming the GP?

Undertaking business activity as a default GP is only part of the process in forming a GP. Other (optional or mandatory) considerations include: reserving and filing a business name with the state or local government (known as a "Doing-Business-As" filing), drafting a partnership agreement, obtaining a business license, registering for a federal EIN and state taxpayer identification number, and obtaining any federal, state or local permits or licenses.

- *Note:* Each state and locality will have specific requirements for businesses carrying on activity in its jurisdiction. Failing to adhere to these requirements can lead to criminal and civil penalties.

Who owns a GP?

The partners are the sole owners of the GP. In the absence of a GP agreement, default partnership rules govern the relationship. By default, partners are entitled to share equally in profits or losses. Further, the default rule is that ownership interests cannot be transferred to third parties without the consent of the existing partners. Attempting an unapproved transfer of an ownership interest is grounds for dissolution of the GP by other partners.

- *Example:* Wayne and Mariah are partners in a dog walking business. Mariah does all of the paperwork and Wayne walks the dogs. Mariah's responsibilities are limited and she only spends about 5 hours per week on the paperwork. Wayne, on the other hand, spends nearly 50 hours per week walking the dogs. The parties have not created a partnership agreement. Under this situation Wayne and Mariah would be default 50/50 owners of the GP. Further, each would be entitled to a 50% interests in all business profits. To change this scenario the parties will need to enter into a partnership agreement either changing the ownership percentage or establishing some special allocation of profits to Wayne.

Who has control and authority to act on behalf of the GP?

In the absence of an agreement otherwise, the default rule is that each partner has an equal voice in the management of the GP. Further, each partner has the authority to act on behalf of the GP. This includes entering into contracts, such as loan agreements, on behalf of the business.

- *Example:* In the scenario above (absent a partnership agreement indicating otherwise), Mariah and Wayne will have equal authority to control the business. If Mariah determines that the business needs to purchase new equipment, she can do so with business funds and without consulting Wayne. Further, if Wayne wishes to modify any of the financial paperwork without consulting Mariah, he can do so as well. Neither party is limited in their job functions and can undertake any function or represent the business in any capacity.

- *Note*: The partners may divide GP interests to designate controlling and minority partners. This is important in GPs that wish to limit the level of authority of any partner. The law of agency applies to partners, who are agents of the GP. See Chapter 3 for additional information on agency law.

What are the partners' duties to the GP?

Partners have default obligations to the GP. As an agent of the GP, these duties are fiduciary in nature. Specifically, a partner has duties of care and loyalty to the GP. The duty of care requires that the partner use reasonable care in carrying out GP business. The duty of loyalty requires that the partner act in the best interest of the GP. This means that the partner cannot usurp any personal benefit that is intended for the GP.

- *Example:* Sally and John are both financial advisors and open a firm together. An investor, Bill, comes in one day and talks to John about serving as his financial advisor and broker. Bill explains that he wants higher returns than the market generally delivers and he wants to know if John is up to the challenge. Further, Bill does not like Sally and does not want any of his funds to be invested by Sally or any percentage of the profits to go to benefit Sally. Bill asks if John can handle his account on the side and not as part of the GP. John, fully aware of his fiduciary duties to the GP, explains to Bill that he cannot usurp a GP business opportunity for his personal gain. Further, he explains that, as partner, he owes a fiduciary duty of care to the GP in carrying out his duties. He cannot make reckless investments in hopes of gaining a higher return, which could subject the GP to disrepute or tort liability.

- *Note:* Partners owe fiduciary duties to the GP. There is generally no duty between partners; however, many courts hold that self-serving conduct at the expense of other parties could violate a partner's duties to the GP.

What is the business continuity in a GP?

Absent a contractual agreement otherwise, partners can leave (dissociate from) the GP at any time. The default rule in many states is that a GP dissolves when a member dissociates. Most states, however, allow the remaining partners to take steps to reform the GP and continue in business after cashing out the dissociating party's interest. One notable exception to the default dissolution rule is when a partner passes away or dissociates by reason of incapacity. In such a case the GP does not automatically dissolve.

- *Example*: Taylor, Will and Mark form a GP. After several months of arduous effort, Mark decides that he is going to dissociate from the GP and seek employment elsewhere. Unless the partnership agreement indicates otherwise, the default rule in many states is that the GP dissolves. Many states would allow Taylor and Will to provide Mark with his share of the GP interest (i.e., cash him out) and make the affirmative decision to continue the GP.

- *Note*: As stated above, the transfer of a GP interest may give rise to a right of dissociation by other partners.

Of course, partners can change the default rules governing the GP by entering into a partnership agreement. For example, the partners can designate a time period for the GP, after which, the GP dissolves. The agreement may also designate the procedures for winding down the business or allowing the remaining partners to continue the business. It can further allocate responsibility for debts of the GP or allocate the proceeds upon dissolution.

- *Note*: Carrying on business as a GP allows for ease of operations, but it is always advisable to have a partnership agreement. One important provision of the agreement is the right of dissolution and the continuity of the venture. As with every business entity, it is important to have a buy-sell agreement in place.

What is a buy-sell agreement and why is it important?

A buy-sell agreement outlines the procedures for a partner leaving the GP. It can be included within the partnership agreement or it can be separate. Generally, it outlines the procedures for dissolving or continuing the business if a partner dissociates. It can outline procedures for both voluntary and mandatory dissociation. It will address the following issues:

- Can a partner be involuntarily expelled?
- When is the GP required to buy out or liquidate a partner's interest?
- What is the process of dividing and liquidating each or all of the partner's interests?
- What method will be used for valuing the business and the dissociating partner's interest?
- Is a dissociating partner able to transfer her GP interest to third parties or is she required to sell her interest back to the GP?
- Is the result different if a party dies? Loses mental capacity? Retires? Involved in a property dispute (such as a divorce), bankruptcy, etc.?

What is the personal liability of the partners?

A GP is similar to a sole proprietorship in that it does not offer the business owners any form of personal liability protection. Each partner is personally liable for any debts, obligations, or tortious conduct of the business. This means that, if the business stops operating or goes bankrupt, the owners are liable for the debts and obligations of the business. In fact, each partner can be held totally liable for the entire debt of the business. This is known as joint and several liability.

- Example: Dawn and Vince are partners in opening a convenience store. The business hires several employees and takes out business loans to fund the venture. One day a customer walks into the store, slips and falls, and subsequently sues the business. As partners Dawn and Vince will be personally liable for all of the business debts and for any tort judgment awarded to the slip-and-fall customer. This means that Dawn and Vince's personal assets (e.g., home, car, bank accounts), as well as the assets of the business, will be at risk for the debts and the torts of the business.

- *Note:* Recall the law of agency from Chapter 3. Every partner is an agent of the GP and will be personally liable for the conduct of any other partner done in the course of business operations. This is true even if one partner exceeds his authority under a partnership agreement. It does not matter if the parties do not realize that they are legally partners.

How are GPs taxed?

GPs are not taxable entities. Like a sole proprietorship, partners report their share of GP profits or losses on their personal income tax returns. The GP does, however, have to prepare a tax return. This return is known as an "informational return" and is filed on IRS Form 1065. The return outlines the revenues and expenses attributable to operations. It will also outline the percentage or amount of the profit or losses to which each party is entitled. The individual partners receive a Form K-1 from the GP outlining their profits or losses from the GP. These amounts are recorded on the owner's individual tax return.

- *Example*: Mike and Mike own a candy store as partners. They share equal control and ownership of the store and there is no special allocation of business profits to either partner. The store brings in $100,000 in revenue with just $80,000 in expenses, producing a $20,000 profit for the year. The GP will have to file an informational return reporting all revenue and expenses. It will also indicate the total profits derived from the business activity. The GP will then produce a Form K-1 that it sends to the IRS, state Department of Revenue, and to the partners. Mike and Mike will each receive a Form K-1 indicating that they received $10,000 in income from the GP. Mike and Mike will then report $10,000 of income on their personal income tax returns. Because it is a pass-through tax entity under Subsection K of the IRC, the GP does not withhold estimated income tax or self-employment taxes from the partners' interests. As such, Mike and Mike will have to pay both income taxes and self-employment taxes on their respective share of the $10,000.

How are partners compensated?

Partners are not entitled to compensation for services rendered to the GP. That is, they do not receive salaries for their services to the GP. Rather, partners generally receive a draw of GP funds at the end of the year. This is known as the partner's distributive share. This draw is often representative of the percentage of ownership of each partner. Absent an agreement outlining the ownership percentage of the partners, each partner is entitled to share equally in the profits and losses of the venture.

- *Example*: In the scenario above, Mike and Mike work equally in the business. As partners they are not entitled to a salary for their work in the GP. Rather, they receive a portion of the profits at the end of the year based upon either their percentage of ownership or some special allocation of profits to either partner. If the GP hires employees who are not owners of the business, these employees will receive a salary from the business. The GP will withhold estimated income taxes as well as payroll taxes from the employees' wages.

- *Note*: GP arrangements are a favorable tax entity for some relationships as profits and losses can usually be allocated in any manner desired. A partner's entitlement to profits or losses does not have to match or be related to the partner's ownership interest in the GP. This is known as a "special allocation" of profits or losses.

What is a special allocation and how does it work?

General partners are not entitled to a salary for services performed for the GP; rather, they receive a distribution or draw of GP proceeds. The default rule is that each partner has equal ownership in the GP and, therefore, shares equally in profits and losses. The parties may, however, allocate the distribution of profits or losses differently from the ownership structure. This must be done through specific provisions in the partnership agreement.

- *Example:* Tom and Erin made equal contributions to the business and share equally in the ownership interest. The business earns money by providing services to clients. While Tom and Erin both provide services to clients, Tom provides additional services to the business that exceed those provided by Erin. As such, Tom and Erin may wish to allocate an additional percentage of the GP profits to Tom to compensate him for the extra effort. In this case, the special allocation of profits to Tom may be justified.

- *Note:* Special allocations are subject to review for validity by the IRS. The business must have a valid justification for a special allocation, other than simply lowering the tax liability of a single party. The IRS employs a "substantial economic effect" test to determine if there is a valid economic reason for the business or the individuals to make special profit or loss allocation.

What is each partner's tax basis?

This is a complicated subject. Entities taxed as GPs have unique basis rules that differ from other entities. Individual partners must track their basis in individual assets within the business. If the assets are later sold by the GP for a gain or loss, then the partner contributing the assets to the business may be attributed income based upon his or her basis in the assets.

In general, tax basis is the value of assets that a partner contributes to the GP; however, this too is an oversimplification. A partner's basis also includes other factors, such as any relief of liability on debt that is assumed by the GP or the amount of business debt for which the partner is personally liable. Remember, it is not necessary that the partner personally guarantee GP debt, as partners are personally liable for any debts of the business. Each partner's basis increases by the product of her percentage ownership in the business multiplied by the amount of debt assumed by the GP. A full discussion of basis calculation for partners is beyond the scope of this text. We strongly advise that you consult a tax professional when making basis calculations for property contributed to a GP.

- *Example*: Tonya invests $1,000 in the GP, so $1,000 is her GP basis. The calculation becomes more complicated if Tonya contributes property to the GP. Suppose instead of cash, Tonya contributes property worth $1,000 to the GP. In that case, she would have the same basis in the stock as she had in the property transferred (adjusted for any debt relief and/or boot). This is known as a "substitute basis". If, however, her basis in the property at the time of contribution was $800, then the property has a built-in gain of $200. IRC Section 721 of the IRC allows for the deferral of any recognition of gain on the property. If, however, the property is later sold by the business for $1,000. The built-in gain will be first taxed to Tonya. If the equipment is later sold for $1,200, the $200 gain is taxed to Tonya and the additional $200 of gain is split between all partners. This simple example is not meant to explain all of the basis rules involved in a GP; rather, it is made to demonstrate the complexity of the topic.

- *Note*: Basis matters for calculation of gains upon sale of the business and for purposes of taxing partnership distributions. When choosing a business entity, it is important to understand the concept of basis and the requirement to track one's basis in assets contributed to a partnership-taxed entity.

What happens if the GP wishes to make a distribution when it is not profitable?

If the GP is not profitable, it may still make a distribution of funds to partners. If the GP distributes an amount of funds to a partner that exceeds the annual profits of the business, then the partner's basis is lowered by that amount. Remember, profits of a GP are counted as personal income to the partners. If the business does not have profits, the partner's distribution is treated as a return of invested capital. Any distribution that reduces a partner's basis below $0, results in taxable income to the partner.

- *Example*: Alex and Virginia own a shoe store as partners. They each have a basis of $10,000 and have not withdrawn any funds other than profits. At the end of the year, the store breaks even and produces no profits. Alex needs money to renovate his home, so he takes a distribution of $5,000 from the GP. Since the business produced no profits, the $5,000 distribution is treated as a return of his capital invested. As such, the distribution is not taxed, but Alex's basis is reduced to $5,000 in the business.

- *Note*: A GP cannot count distributions to partners as business expenses for calculating profits and losses. On the other hand, corporations that pay salaries to shareholder-employees may deduct the salary to these employees as expenses.

What if the partners leave any of the profits in the business, rather than take them out as a distribution?

If the partners decide not to distribute any portion of the GP profits, the percentage of business profits attributable to each partner is still taxable to her. As previously discussed, this is known as "phantom income". The partners report their share of profits on their personal income tax returns, even if it is not actually distributed. The GP now has additional operating funds and the amount of retained funds allocable to a partner raises that partner's basis in the GP.

- *Example*: In the situation above, the following year Alex and Virginia's shoe store makes a profit of $20,000. Neither of the partners is in need of money, so they decide to leave all of the profits in the business with the intent of growing operations. Even though they leave the money in the business, Alex and Virginia will still have to report taxes on $10,000 of the profits on each of their personal income tax returns. Each partner's basis in the business will increase by $10,000.

- *Note*: Phantom income can be a large burden on partners. Because the GP retains the profits, they may not have the personal resources to pay the taxes on their income from the GP activity. For this reason, it is important to address within the partnership agreement the allocation of funds sufficient to cover the partners' tax liability for phantom income.

What happens if the GP suffers losses?

Just like profits, losses pass through to partners and are reported on their personal income tax returns. Since each partner is considered to be actively involved in the GP, the owners can use the losses to offset "active" income earned from other sources. The losses cannot be used to offset passive income.

- *Example*: Winston earns a salary from his day job. He also formed a GP to carry on business with Louise. The GP has lots of expenses and suffers a loss for the tax year. Since this is a GP, Winston can offset these losses against his active income from his day job.

- *Note*: Losses are calculated as income minus expenses. You should familiarize yourself with general accounting principals to determine what is an expense and what is a capital investment.

JOINT VENTURES

What is a joint venture?

Joint ventures operate similarly to GPs, but are specifically formed for a limited purpose or a single project. Unlike a GP, the joint venture does not arise by default through the activity of the joint venturers. Rather, it requires the specific intent of the parties. As such, a joint venture agreement should be in writing to avoid the interpretation of the activity as a GP. Accomplishing a specific goal or working on a specific project is a key characteristic of the joint venture. If the joint venture is repeated, it makes it more likely that a court would interpret the relationship to be a GP. The joint venturers may be individuals or business entities.

- *Example*: Mike owns a fast food restaurant called Mikey's that is organized as an LLC. He has expanded throughout the United States, but now wishes to expend to Canada. He does not know much about the Canadian market, so he approaches a large convenience store chain in Canada called Quick'n Go, Inc. about collaborating to introduce his food service into the Canadian Quick'n Go stores. The parties jointly agree to a two year agreement where Mikey's and Quick'n Go will integrate their businesses and share in the net costs and proceeds. After the two year period, Mikey's will rent the space in Quick'n Go stores. Given the limited time period and nature of the collaboration, this would be a joint venture. Two established businesses have come together for a limited purpose and for a limited time to expand internationally. This is a common scenario employing the joint venture entity form.

- *Note*: Joint ventures are common practices between established business. They are particularly common when one business wishes to expand operations into a new market, such as when expanding sales to a foreign country.

What are the key difference between the joint venture and the GP?

Aside from the limited purpose and time, joint ventures are subject to similar treatment as GPs. Joint venturers owe duties similar to those of partners to the joint venture. These duties are limited, however, by the temporary and targeted nature of the joint venture. Notably, the targeted purpose of the venture may mean that usurping an opportunity that comes about by virtue of the joint venture may not be a breach of duty to the other joint venturers, depending on the nature of the opportunity. The joint venture, by its nature, indicates that the venture does not extend beyond the specific purpose of the venture.

- *Note*: The agency status of joint venturers is not the same as that of a GP. The status as a joint venture limits the scope of each party's authority in acting on behalf of the other parties. The authority inherent in a joint venture relationship is to act within the scope of the entity's limited purpose.

CHAPTER 7: LIMITED PARTNERSHIPS & OTHER HYBRIDS

LIMITED PARTNERSHIP (LP)

What is a LP?

A LP is a common type of business entity recognized under every state's laws. The LP is a form of partnership that includes both limited and general partners, who can be either individuals or businesses. The general partner is governed by GP rules and principals. Limited partners, in contrast, have special rights and duties that are dramatically different from the default partnership rules. Particularly, limited partners receive special treatment regarding control, authority, and taxation. Having limited partners also requires special formation and maintenance requirements.

- *Note*: Every state models its LP law from either the Uniform Limited Partnership Act (ULPA) or its predecessor The Revised Uniform Limited Partnership Act (RULPA). The default rules governing LPs will vary depending upon which of these acts a state most closely observes.

How are LPs created?

Creating a LP requires a written agreement between the partners that indicates the limited partner status of any limited partners. Only one general partner and one limited partner are required; however, there can be numerous limited and general partners. The partners must also file a LP application with the Secretary of State's office. The application must state the purpose of the business and list the name and general contact information for all limited and general partners. If accepted, the Secretary of State will issue a certificate of formation that is filed as a public record either with the Secretary of State's office or in the registrar's office in any locality where the LP operates or does business. The certificate contains the following information: the name of the LP; the character of the business; its location; the name and place of residence of each member; those who are to be the general partners; those who are to be limited partners; the length of time the LP is to exist; the amount of cash or the agreed value of property to be contributed by each partner; and the share of profit or compensation each limited partner shall receive. Given the special role of the limited partner, this public disclosure requirement allows anyone dealing with the LP to understand the makeup of the business.

- *Note*: Identifying the LP status of all limited partners is of primary importance. Many states prohibit the use of a limited partner's name in the title of the LP for fear of public deception. This was the rule under the RULPA. The ULPA eliminates this prohibition. Further, the RULPA requires that the filing documents state the duration of the LP. This requirement is not included in the ULPA.

How is the LP maintained?

The partners must undertake the initial filing process and follow any required updates or filings by the Secretary of State or local registrar's office. This includes updating the records in the event of any change in ownership of the LP, such as the entrance or exit of partners. Further, if a limited partner becomes a general partner, or vice versa, the records must be updated.

Who owns the LP?

The limited and general partners own the LP in whatever percentage is allocated in the LP agreement. Generally, the default partnership rules regarding ownership do not apply, as the LP cannot exist without a LP agreement that allocates ownership interest. Generally, the limited partners provide capital (either funds or physical resources) to the LP, while the general partners provide labor.

- *Example*: Tom agrees to invest $100,000 in a LP with Eric. Eric will be the general partner and run the business. If the partners do not agree otherwise, the default is that each will own 50% of the business. Smartly, the parties draft a LP agreement where Tom will own 60% of the business and Eric will own 40%.

- *Note*: As discussed below, limited partners cannot take part in business operations. Therefore, the limited partner adds value by providing capital to the business. The general partner is not entitled to receive a salary for working in the business, so she generally receives her equity interest in exchange for her management of the LP.

Who has control and authority in a LP?

The terms of the LP agreement control the governance of the organization. There are, however, specific limitations on the authority or ability for limited partners to act. Most notably, limited partners cannot take part in management of the business. This includes any of the actual operations of the business. They cannot exercise control over any activity or anyone carrying out a business activity. The general partner must exercise decision-making authority over all business operations. A limited partner that exceeds this limited authority may lose her limited partner status and be deemed a general partner.

- *Note*: In the scenario above, Tom is the limited partner and will not take part in the decision-making or operations of the business. His limited role will be to advise Eric if he requests it. Eric, as general partner, will run all of the operations and affairs of the business. He can only seek advice from Tom and cannot ask Tom to assist him in running the business. If Tom takes an active part in the business (participates in operations or decision-making) he could be determined to be a general partner if the business is sued by a third-party plaintiff. This means that Tom's personal assets (above the $100,000 invested) would be at risk for the business' tort liability. If all partners lose their limited partner status, the business automatically converts to a GP. The terms of the LP agreement still govern the LP, but the default partnership rules govern any aspect of the LP not specifically addressed within the LP agreement.

What types of activity can the limited partner undertake with respect to the business?

The limited partner may act as an advisor or consultant to the general partner(s), as long as the limited partner has no authority in the decision-making or actions of the general partner. The limited partner may also act as agent or employee of the business, as long as there are strict limitations on the limited partner's control and decision-making. Lastly, the limited partner may undertake other activities to promote the success of the business, such as acting as guarantor of partnership obligations.

- *Note*: If a limited partner takes any of the limited actions described above on behalf of the business, the limited partner's activities should be well documented in order to avoid any claims by third parties that the limited partner is acting as a general partner.

What are the limited partner's rights in the business beyond receiving a percentage of profits?

A limited partner has rights similar to that of an investor in a corporation, but they are generally more extensive given the intimate nature of the LP. Examples of limited partner rights include: inspecting or copying any of the LP records; demanding true and full information about the LP whenever circumstances render just and reasonable; approving or disapproving an amendment to the LP's certificate; voting on matters of fundamental importance such as dissolution, sale of assets, or change of the LP's name; having contribution returned upon dissolution along with any gains in proportion to her ownership interest or as outlined in the LP agreement.

What is the continuity of a LP?

As for continuity, the same rules apply as those of the GP. Since the LP will always have a LP agreement, it generally includes provisions governing the continuity of the business in the event of dissociation by a partner. It will also outline the events that constitute an automatic dissociation event (e.g., personal bankruptcy of a member).

- *Example*: Arni and Doug form a LP where Arni invests $5,000 as limited partner and Doug runs the business as a general partner. Doug decides to leave or dissociate from the LP. Since Doug is a general partner, the LP dissolves and each party is entitled to the value of her ownership in the business. Arni decides to buy out Doug's interest and continue the business operations. The LP is now dissolved and Arni is a sole proprietor.

- *Note*: The right of a limited partner to dissociate varies under the ULPA and RULPA. Under the RULPA a limited partner can withdraw from the LP upon six-months notice. Under the ULPA there is no provision for the dissociation of the limited partner prior to the termination of the LP. Further, under the RULPA, dissolution of the LP requires unanimous written consent of the partners. Under the ULPA only the written consent of all general partners and the written consent of a majority of the limited partners, if those limited partners collectively hold a majority interest in the partnership.

What personal liability protection does a LP offer?

A limited partner has limited liability for debts and torts of the LP. Specifically, the limited partner is only personally liable for LP liabilities to the extent of her investment in the business.

General partners, on the other hand, face unlimited personal liability. Remember, actively participating in management will cause the limited partner to be treated as a general partner. This means losing the limited liability protection and risking one's personal assets for debts of the business.

- *Example*: Sarah and Ashley have a LP. Sarah is the limited partner and has invested $10,000 in the business. Ashley is a general partner and runs the daily affairs of the business. Joey sues the business for a faulty product manufactured and sold by the LP. Ashley as general partner will be personally liable for the debts and tort liability of the business. Sarah is a limited partner and will not be personally liable, though the value of her business interest may reduce to zero ($0). If the business has insufficient funds to satisfy a judgment against the business, Joey may seek to attack Sarah's status as a limited partner. If he can show the court that Sarah acted as a general partner (e.g., took part in business decision-making or operations) then he may be able to execute the judgment on her personal assets.

- *Note*: Under the ULPA, a limited partner cannot be held liable for the LP debts even if she participates in the management and control of the LP. Under the RULPA, however, a limited partner may be held personally liable for certain debts of the business that exceed her investment.

How is a LP taxed?

LPs are taxed similarly to a GP. The profits and losses of the LP pass through to the owners and are reported on the owners' personal income tax statements. The LP must file a LP return, which is an informational return that indicates the amount of business profits, losses, etc. The LP must provide a Form K-1 to partners indicating the amount of profits or losses allocated to the partner. While a general partner's distributive share is always considered active income, the limited partner is subject to active and passive loss rules. The profits and losses distributed to her are passive in nature if she does not materially participate in the business venture.

- *Example*: Reggie and Stephanie are partners in a LP. Reggie is the limited partner and Stephanie is the general partner. They share equally in ownership and there is no special allocation of profits. At the end of the year, the LP has $10,000 in profit. Like a GP, the LP will file an informational return with the IRS and submit a Form K-1 to Reggie and Stephanie indicating their share. The Form K-1 will also indicate whether Reggie and Stephanie are active or passive participants in the business. Since Reggie is a passive investor, his profits are passive while Stephanie's profits are active. Recall that active profits can offset only active losses and passive profits can offset only passive losses.

- *Note*: Limited partners receive one substantial advantage in that their allocation of LP profits are not subject to self-employment tax (15.6% in 2014). The general partners must pay self-employment tax on their proceeds.

Where are LPs most commonly used?

LPs are far less common in small businesses since the inception of the LLC. The LP is, however, very common in certain industries, such as real estate investment and venture capital or private equity firms. The LP is especially useful when there is high need for flexibility in entity maintenance and governance, while allowing for limited liability protection and limited control for investors.

- *Note*: LPs often include numerous general partners that are business entities themselves.

LIMITED LIABILITY PARTNERSHIPS (LLP)

What is a LLP?

A LLP is a specialty entity recognized in most states. It is a hybrid entity that has characteristics similar to a GP, but has limited liability protections similar to that of an LLC (discussed in detail in Chapter 8).

- *Note*: Many states limit the type of businesses that can operate as LLPs.

How is the LLP created?

The LLP requires the filing of an application with the Secretary of State's office. The form requires all of the information found in a LP application. Existing GPs or LPs can convert into a LLP through this method. This will generally require significant modification to the LLP agreement to include the necessary information. Other requirements may include a description of the business and a certification that the business will obtain liability insurance.

- *Note:* States may restrict the LLP entity to certain professions, such as accountants, attorneys, doctors, or other professional service providers.

Who owns a LLP?

The partners own an interest in the LLP as outlined in the LLP agreement. Like a GP, the agreement can allocate ownership in any manner. Further, it can make special allocations of profits and losses, subject to similar tests for economic significance.

Who controls the LLP?

Unlike a LP, each partner has the ability to exercise control within the LLP. LLPs are often created to protect partners from liability for the professional malpractice of other partners. In this form each partner has little control over the activities of the other partners.

- *Note:* The LLP agreement may designate partner seniority and managing partners who control the administration functions of the LLP.

What is the continuity of the LLP?

The continuity of the LLP is similar to that of a GP. Since there must be a LLP agreement, it normally outlines the process or procedure for dissociation by any partner.

- *Note*: In the absence of provisions covering dissociation in the LLP agreement, the default LP rules apply. Under certain conditions the dissociation by a partner may give cause for other partners to dissociate. Dissociation of a partner would not necessarily give rise to dissolution of the entity.

What limited liability protection does the LLP offer?

Each partner receives limited liability protection with regard to the actions of other partners. The LLP assets are subject to liability for the debts of the LLP and for the tortious actions of any partner, employee, or other agent of the business. However, the personal assets of each partner are protected from liability from the actions of others. This relationship allows the partners to enjoy the freedoms and lack of formality associated with a LLP along with the limited liability protection of other entity forms.

- *Note:* A partner (in any type of partnership) is always personally liable for her own actions. Further, some states limit the liability protection of limited liability partners to negligence actions. In such cases, the other partners are still personally liable for debts of the LLP and intentional conduct of other partners.

How is a LLP taxed?

LLPs are taxed similarly to a GP. Profits and losses pass through to the partner based upon her share of the ownership or in accord with the special allocation provisions of the LLP agreement.

- *Note*: Generally, each limited liability partner is treated as a general partner. As such, income received from the LLP business activity is considered active income. This also means that income imputed to the partners is subject to self-employment taxes.

When is a LLP used?

The LLP form is popular with professional services firms, such as accountants, architects, and lawyers. The reason is because of the extensive potential liability associated with their services. A partner in a professional services firm will not want to be personally liable for the malpractice of other partners.

- *Note*: The limited personal liability of partners leads to the requirement by many states that the LLP or the individual partners obtain insurance policies that cover malpractice.

LIMITED LIABILITY LIMITED PARTNERSHIPS (LLLP)

What is a LLLP?

A LLLP is a unique business entity recognized by multiple states. This entity combines features of the LP and the LLP. Like a LP, the LLLP includes limited partners and general partners.

How is a LLLP created?

The LLLP is created in the same manner as a LP. It requires an application to the Secretary of State's office containing all of the information requirements of the LP and LLP.

- *Note:* Some states, such as Delaware, simply require the election of LLLP status at the time of filing a LLP application.

Who owns the LLLP?

Each partner owns an interest in the LLLP as outlined in the LLLP agreement. The limited partners generally provide capital to the business in exchange for their ownership interest. The other partners, while receiving limited liability protection, are treated as general partners.

Who controls the LLLP?

As in a LP, the limited partners in the LLLP cannot take part in the management or control of the business. The general partners manage and control the operations of the business. The nature of business operations has characteristics that necessitate the personal liability protection of general partners.

- *Note*: The partners will always be subject to personal liability for their own actions.

What is the continuity of the LLLP?

Continuity in a LLLP is similar to that of a LP. If the limited partners leave the LLLP, then the general partners can elect to continue on as a GP or dissolve the LLLP. If all of the general partners exit the LLLP, then it is dissolved.

- *Note*: Dissociation is generally controlled by the LLLP agreement. Dissociation by any partner may give rise to a right of dissolution under the state's default rules.

How is the LLLP taxed?

The LLLP is taxed similarly to a GP. Each partners receives a distribution or draw of LLLP profits. The LLLP must file an informational return with the IRS and each partner receives a Form K-1 from the LLLP indicating their share. Like a GP, the LLLP can have special allocations that meet the economic significance test. The limited partners will be subject to active and passive loss rules.

Where is the LLLP commonly used?

LLLPs are common in professional ventures that are of interest to outside investors, but require the flexibility in governance and operations of the GP form. This type of entity is most common in real estate deals. The general partners seek limited personal liability for actions with respect to the real estate investment, but they need the investment capital from limited partners.

- *Note*: The LLLP entity form may fit a number of unique types of business activity. CNN is probably the best known LLLP.

What is the personal liability of LLLP partners?

Each partner has limited personal liability for the debts and torts of the LLLP or other partners.

CHAPTER 8: LIMITED LIABILITY COMPANIES

What is a limited liability company (LLC)?

A LLC is a state recognized entity that blends the characteristics of a GP and a corporation. The primary characteristics of a LLC are flexibility in governance, tax liability similar to that of a GP, and limited liability for the members similar to that of corporations.

- *Note:* The LLC has quickly become the most popular business entity form in the United States for small businesses with more than one owner.

How is a LLC created?

An LLC is created by filing articles of organization with the Secretary of State's office. The organizer must be an individual and cannot be a corporation. There must be at least one member of the LLC. If it is only one, it is known as a "single-member LLC". Like other entity filings, the Secretaries of State charge filing fees for registration.

- *Note:* Some states require businesses to publish notice of intent to create an LLC. Notice is generally achieved by publishing notice in a local newspaper.

What must be included in the articles of organization?

The articles of organization is a simple document containing basic information about the business activity and the organizers. The articles must contain the name of the business (ending in "LLC"); the business address; the name of the organizer; the name, address, and contact information for a registered agent; and the business purpose. You may record the names of the members or managers if known at the time. Finally, you will need to choose whether the LLC is member-managed or manager-managed (discussed below) and how the LLC chooses to be taxed (as a partnership or corporation - discussed below). Individual states may require additional information.

- *Note:* As with other business entities, you should make certain that your chosen business name is available. That is, you must make certain another business in the state is not already using your intended business name. Most Secretary of State websites have a search function allowing you to check the availability of names. If you determine the name you want is available, you can reserve it prior to registration. This will keep others from using the name in the interim. Just because a business name is available, however, does not mean that it does not infringe on someone's trademark. You should conduct a thorough search to make certain using a given name is legal.

What are the LLC maintenance requirements?

Maintenance requirements in an LLC are minimal. The business is not required to have annual meetings. The LLC operating agreement controls the governance and internal operations of the

LLC, such as holding meetings, voting rights, keeping of records, etc. At a bare minimum, LLCs must update the corporate records when any major changes take place in the business. This includes changing registered agents, moving addresses, discontinuing operations, etc.

- *Note*: The limited maintenance requirements are a big draw of the LLC over other pass-through tax entities that offer limited liability, such as the S corporation.

What is an operating agreement?

The operating agreement is the governing document for an LLC. It serves a purpose similar to the bylaws in a corporation and the partnership agreement in a partnership. The unique aspect of the operating agreement is, like the partnership agreement, it allows a great deal of flexibility in organizing the governance of the LLC. The operating agreement lays out all of the material provisions for governing the business. Common provisions include:

- Outlining each owner's interest in the LLC,
- Rules for the transfer of LLC interest,
- The rights of each member,
- The authority of members,
- How the LLC will be managed,
- Allocation of business profits and losses,
- Voting rights and procedures,
- Requirements for meetings and records, and
- Rules for the entrance and exit of members.

State law does not require that an LLC have an operating agreement, but it is a very good idea to have one. States have default rules that control the governance of the LLC and the relationships between the LLC members. These rules are comprehensive, but they often do not adequately represent the intentions of the parties.

How can a business change into an LLC?

Sole proprietorships and GPs can easily convert into an LLC by filing articles of organization. The parties then terminate or dissolve the prior business and transfer the assets to the LLC. The Secretary of State's office prescribes the appropriate documents for any entity type to covert into an LLC. Many offices have standard forms called certificates of conversion to effectuate the conversion.

- *Note*: Corporations are more complicated entities and much care should be taken in converting the entity into an LLC. Converting the entity will necessarily affect the rights of shareholders, the authority of managers, and the relationship with third parties. Further, converting a business entity can have significant tax consequences for the business and its owners. Because the ownership and management structure of a corporation is far more detailed, you should consult a legal and tax professional when considering converting an entity. When converting a business entity, you will need to take care to transfer all incidental aspects of the business, such as building permits, licenses, leases, etc.

Who owns the LLC?

The equity owners of an LLC are known as members. LLCs do not have shareholders; however, members hold membership units that are very similar to equity shares.

- *Example*: Will and Grace organize their business as an LLC. They will each own the business and have the title as members. Will holds 60% ownership and Grace owns 40% of the business. In an operating agreement, Will and Grace will authorize a certain number of membership units (e.g., 100). They will then allocate these units among the members as desired (e.g., 60 units to Will and 40 units to Grace).

- *Note*: There is generally only one class of equity ownership in the LLC. There are, however, innovative ways of using contracts to provide additional rights and duties between the owners. A common form of special allocation of contractual rights is "profits-only interest", which provides a right to share in profits but does not entail traditional ownership rights.

Who has control over the LLC?

Members make an election at the time of organization whether the business will be member-managed or manager-managed. Member-managed LLCs are very similar to GPs. The default rule is that each member has equal authority to manage or act on behalf of the business. As such, members should take great care to outline the authority and rights of members in the operating agreement. Manager-managed LLCs are organized more like a corporation. The members retain the authority to vote for major business decisions, but the manager(s) run the business and control the daily affairs. In such an entity, the members do not have the authority to control or act on behalf of the business.

- *Example*: Tom, Dick, and Shirley start a private detective business together and organize as an LLC. Tom and Dick will run the business and act as investigators. Shirley is simply a passive investor in the business. They will share any profits equally, but Tom and Dick will also earn a salary for their services to the LLC. In order to effectuate this plan, they organize as a manager-managed LLC. Tom and Dick are managers and members, while Shirley is just a member. Tom and Dick will have all of the managerial authority, while Shirley has the right to vote on major business decisions and to receive her share of annual LLC profits.

- *Note*: The operating agreement should be used to allocate control in a member-managed or manager-managed LLC. Failing to do so risks business liability for the actions of individuals who do not have authority to act on behalf of the business. See Chapter 3 "Agency and Liability" for more information.

How are members of an LLC compensated?

Compensation for LLC members depends on whether the LLC is member-managed or manager-managed. Members of a member-managed LLC are not entitled to compensation for their services to the LLC. Rather, they receive a distribution of LLC profits based upon their ownership percentage in the business. Like partnerships, LLCs can allow for special allocations to LLC members. Again, these allocations are subject to the substantial economic effect test. In a manager-managed LLC, on the other hand, managers receive a salary for their services to the LLC. Their salary is in addition to any distribution of LLC profits commensurate with their percentage of ownership or special allocation.

- *Example*: In the scenario above, Tom and Dick will receive a salary for their services to the LLC manager-managed firm. After all expenses are paid, including Tom and Dick's salaries, the profits will be distributed to the LLC members in their respective ownership percentage or pursuant to a special allocation.

- *Note*: Manager-managed LLCs treat the managers as employees of the business and the non-manager members more like passive investors.

What is the continuity of an LLC?

An LLC is a separate entity from its owners. The business continues until there is an act of dissolution by the owners. Dissociation of a member may or may not be grounds for dissolution. Like a GP, default rules restrict the transfer of LLC interests to outside parties. If a party seeks to transfer her interest or dissociate from the entity, then it is grounds for dissolution of the entity by the other parties. The business dissolves if a member dissociates from the firm, unless the other parties decide to continue the business within a statutory period of time. Dissolution requires a winding up of the business. This includes the settling of debts and the distribution of ownership interest to the parties. Most LLCs do not depend upon the default rules and address continuity within the operating agreement or within a separate buy-sell agreement. These documents will outline what constitutes events giving rise to dissolution.

- *Note*: Common events that are grounds for dissolution of the entity include: bankruptcy of a member, retirement, death or incapacity, a divorce dispute, loss of a professional license, etc. The operating agreement or other governance documents will further control the transfer of ownership, redemption rights for the members, rights of first refusal by the business, valuation of the interest, and other procedures and terms for the dissociation of a partner.

What limited personal liability protection does the LLC offer?

An important characteristic of LLCs is that the members do not face personal liability for the debts of the business entity. Members and employees are, however, agents of the LLC itself. Their actions subject the LLC to potential liability in contract and tort. The benefit of limited personal liability protection is that individual owners are shielded from personal liability created by other members or employees. Remember, an individual is always liable for her own conduct. The limited liability protections of the business entity do not protect against personal liability of one's own actions.

- *Example*: Winston and Salem form a member-managed LLC that sells cigarettes to local convenience stores. During one of his deliveries, Winston crashed into a pedestrian and injured her. She subsequently sues Winston and the LLC. Winston is potentially liable because it was his conduct that hurt the pedestrian. The LLC is potentially liable under a theory of vicarious liability, as Winston is an agent of the LLC. Salem, however, will be able to avoid personal liability for the actions of Winston. Salem still runs the risk of the plaintiff attacking the LLC entity form for failure to maintain business formalities.

- *Note*: While limited liability is a primary reason for choosing the LLC as an operating structure, it is the subject of a great deal of confusion among business owners. The misunderstanding regards the extent of limited liability afforded by forming an LLC.

How can an LLC member lose personal liability protection?

Personal liability protection is based upon the presumption that the business entity is completely separate from its members. Members who fail to maintain business formalities demonstrating this separation may lose their personal liability protection. This is known as "piercing the veil" and is discussed further in the context of corporations.

- *Example*: In the scenario above, suppose Winston and Salem fail to maintain business formalities. For example, they regularly right checks out of the business bank account to pay for their personal expenses. Further, the business is under-capitalized to support operations and there is no insurance policy to cover potential claims against the business. If this is the case, the plaintiff pedestrian may be able to overcome the LLC's liability shield and hold Salem personally liable for the tortious conduct of the business.

- *Note*: The considerations for when a court will pierce the veil of liability protection and subject the owners to personal liability for the debts of the business are similar for corporations and LLCs. The primary method of losing this protection is by failing to adequately maintain a separation between personal and business funds.

When is an LLC owner personally liable (other than when the court pierces the veil)?

The limited liability afforded by the business entity protects members from liability arising from the business and from the conduct of others. As with other business entities, LLC members are always personally liable for their own tortious conduct. Further, LLC members often guarantee loans made to the LLC. If the LLC defaults, the LLC member will be personally liable. Lastly, an LLC member may be liable to the LLC for conduct outside her authority that causes liability for the business. That is, the LLC may be able to bring an action against the member to recover for losses caused by the member's conduct.

- *Example*: Continuing on the previous example, Winston is potentially personally liable for crashing into the pedestrian. The LLC entity status does not protect him from liability arising from his own conduct. Further, the LLC will be vicariously liable for Winston's actions because the tort was committed in the scope of employment. The LLC only insulates other LLC owners from personal liability for the debts and torts of the business (including its agents), but cannot protect a person from their own conduct.

- *Note*: The above example discusses liability for the tortious activity of the business or its agent. Liability for debts of the business is different. The LLC entity status may protect an individual for the debts of the business. An individual who incurs a debt on behalf of the business is not personally liable for the debt, even though she may have signed the agreement on behalf of the LLC to incur the debt. Review Chapter 3 on agency law for a discussion of exceeding the scope of one's authority.

How are LLCs taxed?

LLCs, like partnerships, are pass-through tax structures (unless the members choose to be taxed as a corporation). The tax regime for LLC members is very similarly to that of partners, except for a few notable exceptions discussed below. Any profits of the business pass through and are recorded on the member's tax return. The LLC must complete an informational return demonstrating the profits or losses of the business and the allocation to members. The business must also provide a Form K-1 to the partners indicating their share of profits or losses. While the law is being developed, members of member-managed LLCs generally do not t pay self-employment taxes on their distributions. Managers in manager-managed LLCs receive wages from the LLC. The LLC must withhold payroll taxes and the manager must pay FICA taxes. Further, the manager must pay self-employment taxes on any distribution from the LLC, because the income is considered "active income."

- *Example*: Craig and Jeff are co-owners of a consulting firm that is organized as an LLC. The LLC has several employees and other operational expenses. At the end of the year the firm made a profit of $100,000. The LLC will have to file an informational return demonstrating all revenue and expenses. It will also indicate the amount of profits attributable to each owner. Craig and Jeff will receive a K-1 from the LLC indicating their share of the business profits. This amount will be reported on their individual tax returns.

- *Note*: Currently non-managing members generally do not pay self-employment taxes on distributions, because their status if very similar to that of limited partners in a LP.

Are LLC distributions treated as active or passive income?

This is an on-going issue between courts and the IRS. The IRS has proposed the treatment of certain non-managing LLC members as passive investors subject to the passive activity rules. Courts have not yet adopted this stance and have held that LLC members should apply the test for material participation in determining whether losses are active or passive.

- *Example*: In the scenario above, assume Craig is an active member of the LLC and the sole manager of the firm. Craig earns a salary from the firm for his services as manager. Jeff is mostly a passive investor who seeks to receive a share of the firm's total profits. If the court holds that Jeff has done enough to be considered a material participant, all compensation (salary or share of earnings) received by Craig and Jeff is considered active income. Unlike a LP, where Jeff's share of profits would be assumed to be passive income, in an LLC all profits may be determined to be active income to the owners.

- *Note:* Tax planners generally treat LLC members who do not materially participate in operations as passive investors.

What activities affect the owner's basis in the LLC?

Unlike the GP, loans to the LLC do not necessarily increase the LLC owner's basis. There is limited room for an increase in at-risk basis for LLC members who personally guarantee loans to the LLC. The IRS has taken the stance that, when there is more than one personal guarantor of a business, then personally guaranteeing a loan to the business does not increase one's at-risk basis.

- *Example*: Continuing the scenario above, Craig's basis in the business is $10,000 and Jeff's basis is $20,000. These amounts reflect the initial capital invested in the business by each LLC member. Craig later personally guarantees a loan to the business for $10,000. This may raise Craig's basis to $20,000 because he is the loan guarantor. If, however, Jeff also guarantee's the loan, then the IRS may disallow an increase in the at-risk basis of either member.

- *Note*: The rule that joint personal guarantees of a loan do not increase an LLC owner's basis is different from the rule in a GP. This is another topic that is subject to dispute and may be a common point of contention in the future.

CHAPTER 9: CORPORATIONS

What is a corporation?

A corporation is one of the earliest forms of legally recognized business entity. Corporations exist under every state's laws. The corporation is the most formalized and developed form of business entity. Its structure is developed to optimize the relationship between owners (shareholders), high level decision-makers (Directors), and operational managers (Executives).

- *Note*: The rights of a corporation have consistently expanded in recent years. For example, the US Supreme Court has determined that corporations are legal persons and have rights similar to those of individuals.

How is the corporation created?

The state issues a charter upon the application of individuals known as incorporators. The application for a corporate charter is known as filing the articles of incorporation. Once the corporate charter is issued, the incorporator must take actions to form the board of directors. Once the board is formed, it must act to ratify the incorporator's actions, adopt the bylaws, and approve a variety of corporate actions (including the distribution of stock to owners).

- *Note*: Chapter 12 reviews the major internal steps necessary to set up the corporate entity.

What is included in the articles of incorporation?

The articles of incorporation serve as the charter for the business. As such, it must contain the primary information about the business, including:

- The name of the business,
- The name and address of the incorporators,
- The corporate purpose (nature of business),
- The duration of the business (generally perpetual),
- The name and address of a registered agent, and
- The information about the stock being issued (number of shares, the classes of shares, and the value of each share).

- *Note*: Many states require that the filing be advertised in the local newspaper for a stated period of time to make the public aware of the filing.

What are the corporate bylaws and why do they matter?

The bylaws is a single document containing the governance provisions controlling the business operations and the relationships between those involved in the business. The incorporators generally write or construct the bylaws prior to forming the business. As such, the initial directors can adopt the bylaws at the first meeting. The primary issues addressed in the bylaws include:

- Demographic information about the corporation,
- The number of directors,
- The method for electing directors,
- The number of classes of equity shares authorized,
- The requirements for director and shareholder meetings,
- The requirements for corporate record-keeping, and
- The procedures for amending the charter or bylaws.

- *Note*: Most states do not require that the bylaws be publicly filed, but they must be maintained at the business's place of record. This is important as shareholders are generally entitled to access to and review of the corporate records.

How are corporations maintained?

The amount of formality associated with corporate maintenance increases with the size of the business. For example, large C corporations have extensive requirements for maintaining the business (meetings, voting requirements, etc.), while closely-held corporations have special exemptions from the extensive maintenance requirements. Most of the reporting requirements for a corporation are to the shareholders under state law or to the general public under the federal laws.

- *Note*: State's vary in their updated filing requirements for the corporation. The requirements generally include information about the current corporate officials, the principal place of business, the registered agent, etc.

Like other business entities, management must maintain formalities to avoid challenges to the corporate entity status. The most important of these formalities is keeping corporate assets separate from individual assets. Another maintenance formality includes keeping detailed records of all actions taken. This is normally done through director and shareholder meetings or through consents. Both directors and shareholders must hold annual meetings. Consents are actions approved in writing by directors or shareholders outside of meetings. Most states require that directors undertake major actions of the corporation during an annual or special meeting. Directors generally hold special meetings throughout the year to deal with special issues. At meetings directors and shareholders act through resolutions that are documented by the corporate secretary.

- *Note*: A corporation must generally have at least one officer - the corporate secretary. She is responsible for documenting the formal transaction of the board or shareholders during meetings. Often a small corporation will have few officers and one individual may hold several positions.

How do these requirements change for small and closely-held corporations (such as startup ventures)?

Closely-held corporations can avoid much of the formality associated with larger and publicly held corporations. Many states have statutes specifically allowing for lesser formalities. Often these businesses will have only a few shareholders who also serve as directors and officers. A corporation can have as few as one owner. The one shareholder can serve as director and officer of the corporation. In fact, the shareholder can appoint herself to fulfill all roles for the company. Absent a statutory exemption, however, small corporations must still comply with many of the corporate formalities to avoid attacks on the corporate entity status.

- *Example*: Rachel and Keith form a corporation pursuant to a state statute allowing for closely-held corporations. Rachel and Keith act as shareholders, directors, and officers of the business. The state statute allows for Keith and Rachel to hold all of these positions. It also requires far less formalities than a typical corporation. For example, the statute could allow Rachel and Keith to not hold regular meetings or to not keep strict meeting minutes.

- *Note*: The important point is that a shareholder who holds positions as officer and director must closely observe the formalities in decision-making pursuant to each responsibility and document her actions accordingly.

Why do many businesses incorporate in Delaware?

Many corporations choose Delaware as the state of incorporation for a number of reasons, including: ease of formation, an established body of corporate law, chancery courts to adjudicate disputes, no state income tax on corporations that do not carry on business within the state, and a generally corporate friendly legal system and legislators. The chancery court and the thoroughly established body of corporate law are the primary reasons for incorporating in Delaware. This provides a level of comfort or certainty in carrying on business.

- *Note*: This topic is discussed further in Chapter 14.

Who owns the corporation?

Corporations are owned by shareholders. Closely-held corporations are held by a small group of shareholders. Non-publicly traded corporations may be more widely held, but shares are not traded on a public exchange. Public corporation shares are publicly traded on exchanges (or in over-the-counter transactions) and are often very widely held. The shareholders are entitled to receipt of any profits of the corporation upon sale or liquidation (after all liabilities are paid). Shareholders may be divided into classes, depending upon the type of shares they own. Most commonly, a corporation will issue two types of shares: common and preferred. Common and preferred shareholders often have different levels of entitlement.

- *Example*: Lawrence purchase shares of common stock of Apple, Inc. He is now an owner of the company. He has the right to vote those shares for the election of corporate directors and for the decision to undertake major corporate actions (such as a merger or dissolution).

- *Note*: The ownership structure of a corporation can be very complex. Corporate boards often authorize various types of preferred shares that carry specific rights. These shares are used to seek certain types of investors or to assure control to certain shareholders. For example, a single preferred share may have 100 votes for directors, where a common share has only one vote.

Who has authority or controls the corporation?

Responsibilities within a corporation are divided among three groups:

- Shareholders (owners)
- Directors (high level managers)
- Officers (daily operations managers).

What is the authority of shareholders?

Common shareholders (and sometimes preferred shareholders) have two primary types of authority. First, shareholders vote to elect the board of directors. Second, shareholders must approve any major corporate actions (e.g., amending the articles of incorporation, increasing authorized shares, adding new classes of shares, dissolving the corporation, entering into a merger, and some stock repurchases). Some of these decisions also require director approval (or at least initiation).

What is the authority of the board of directors?

Directors make high-level and strategic management decisions for the corporation. Basically, the board makes all material decisions that are outside of the ordinary course of business operations. For example, director approval is required for issuing shares, granting options, entering into very large contracts, opening new lines of credit, appointing new corporate officers, purchasing another business, dissolution of the corporation.

- *Note*: Some director responsibilities are must be proposed by directors and approved by shareholder vote.

What is the authority of officers?

Officers are in charge of the daily affairs of the corporation. They account for all business activity not reserved for the directors and shareholders.

- *Example*: Terry is appointed by the board of directors as Chief Executive Officer (CEO) of the GoodBiz, Inc. She is now in charge of all business operations. All subordinate managers and employees will report to her and she will report to the board of directors. In many corporations Terry will also serve on the board.

- *Note*: Many of the requirements for shareholder and board approval are outlined in the bylaws. In some cases, the shareholders or directors will vote to add governance requirements to the articles of incorporation.

What is the continuity of the corporation?

A corporation exists independently of its owners. Unless the owners undertake an act of dissolution, the corporation will continue to exist. Notably, dissociation by shareholders, directors, or officers of a corporation is not grounds for dissolution. Generally, shareholders may sell or exchange their corporate interest and the business entity continues to exist. Unlike other forms of business entity, corporations have continuity by default. If desired, shareholders may vote to add dissolution provisions to the articles of incorporation or bylaws.

- *Example*: Amy, Jean, and Violet form a corporation. Each is a shareholder, serves as a director, and holds a position as corporate officer. If any one of them decides to leave the business, then the corporation does not dissolve. At this point it is important to have bylaws that address the issue of a shareholder leaving a closely held corporation. The bylaws will determine the rules for dissolution and the procedures by which a shareholder may dissociate. Further, it will determine the mechanism by which the dissociating individual resigns their positions as officer and/or director.

- *Note*: Closely-held corporations or corporations that issue restricted shares should have detailed buy-sell agreements. Corporate buy-sell agreements will contain the same provisions as LLC buy-sell agreement. They generally provide investors with liquidity through redemption rights and allow the corporation to control the distribution of shares through rights of first refusal. Buy-Sell agreements generally address: who can buy shareholder stock; under what conditions the company must repurchase shareholder stock; how to value the stock; payment terms in the event of buyout; events that give rise to a duty to buy or sell stock; etc. Examples of events possibly giving rise to dissolution include: death, incapacity, personal bankruptcy, divorce, termination of employment in the business, etc.

What is the extent of limited liability protection in a corporation?

All parties have limited personal liability for the debts and torts of the corporation. Shareholders are only liable to the extent of their investment in the corporation. Assets of the corporation can be used to satisfy such debts, which may decrease the value of the shareholder's equity. Directors and officers are generally not liable for actions taken in the course of business; however, both may be subject to shareholder suits for any actions (or approval of actions) that damage the corporation. These suits are known as "derivative shareholder actions". In this type of action, shareholders sue the directors or officers on behalf of the corporation.

- *Example*: Mary is the CEO and a director of ABC, Inc. She decides to purchase a corporate jet with business funds to make it easier for her to travel to business meetings. The shareholders are angered by her purchase and bring a shareholder's derivative action against her for waste of corporate funds. Mary will be protected by what is called "the business judgment rule" if her decision to purchase the jet with business funds was a reasonable decision. If, however, her decision was reckless or grossly negligent, then she could be held personally liable for the expenditure.

- *Note*: The business judgment rule provides that an officer or director may only be held liable for their bad faith conduct. Bad faith conduct includes intentional misconduct or self-serving conduct.

How can a shareholder lose limited liability protection?

Shareholders risk losing limited liability protection by court order. As previously mentioned, a plaintiff may sue the corporate shareholder(s) alleging that the court should "pierce the corporate veil" and hold shareholders liable for corporate debt (or civil liability). This claim involves the "alter ego theory". Under the alter ego theory, shareholders who fail to maintain established corporate formalities risk losing their limited liability protections. Such a failure demonstrates that the purpose of the business entity is not to carry on business as a separate entity; rather, the corporate entity is simply a shell used for limited liability purposes. The court will ask the following questions in evaluating whether to pierce the corporate veil:

- Did the business maintain business formalities, such as organizational filings, meeting minutes, etc.?
- Did the business owners intermingle personal and business funds or other assets?
- Is the business adequately capitalized or does it have adequate liability protection in place?
- Does the history of distribution of funds to owners show an intent to drain entity funds?
- Did business members comply with or routinely deviate from their roles and responsibilities?

- *Note*: If the court is convinced that the shareholders have misused the corporate form, it will be disregarded for liability purposes.

- *Example*: Bill, Joye, and Thomas form a corporation. The corporation remains closely held by the three founders. They fail to hold regular meetings. They do not document many of their corporate actions. Further, they often pay corporate debts from their personal bank accounts and their personal debts from business bank accounts. If a plaintiff sues the corporation, it is possible that a court would disregard the corporate entity status and subject Bill, Joye, and Thomas to personal liability for any tortious activity or debts of the business.

How are corporations taxed?

Corporations pay income taxes on their net profits. This is known as entity-level taxation. Salaries to employees or payments to contractors are expenses to the corporation that are deducted from income. After-tax distributions of profits to shareholders (dividends) are taxed again to the shareholder. This is known as double taxation. Certain corporations may avoid paying taxes at the entity level and pass the tax obligation through to its shareholders.

As stated above, corporations may choose to be either: 1) taxed as a pass-through entity or 2) to be subject to double taxation. Pass-through taxation is achieved pursuant to subchapter S of the IRC. If the corporation meets the necessary qualifications, it can elect to be taxed under subchapter S on a pass-through basis. The corporation is commonly referred to as an S corporation. If the corporation fails to qualify under subchapter S, or it does not make an "S election", it will be subject to double taxation under Subchapter C of the IRC. The type of corporation is referred to as a C corporation.

- *Note*: Review Chapter 4 for additional information on double taxation and pass-through taxation.

What are the requirements to qualify as an S corporation?

To qualify for S corporation status, the business must be a corporation organized in the United States. All shareholders must be U.S. Citizens or resident aliens. It cannot have more than 100 shareholders. All members of a family are considered to be one investor for purposes of this rule. All shareholders must be individuals, trusts, or certain other exempt organizations. The company may only authorize one class of stock (common stock). The company must follow an accepted tax year. Finally, all shareholders must consent to the S-election.

- *Note*: It is fairly easy to run afoul of the S corporation requirements and lose the status. A business may exceed the number of eligible shareholders, accidentally transfer an interest in the business to a business entity, or authorize what is deemed a second class of shares. Certain banking and insurance companies are not eligible for S corporation status.

Are there any ways to be a C corporation and avoid double taxation?

Corporations often avoid double taxation by not paying a dividend. Profits will still be subject to a corporate tax rate, but not taxed as income to the individual. The problem with this approach is that the shareholder does not receive any of the profits; rather, she enjoys capital appreciation of her stock. Another method for avoiding double taxation is paying higher salaries to shareholder employees. This means that the shareholder will pay ordinary income tax on the income. Further, the corporation will have to pay payroll taxes on the salary. The corporation will deduct any salaries paid as corporate expenses. Depending on the tax rate of the corporation and individual, this arrangement may still save money above paying a corporate income tax and individual dividend tax.

- *Example*: Mike invests money in XYZ, Inc., a C corporation. The corporation is profitable at the end of the year, producing $50,000 in profits. The corporation will have to pay taxes on the $50,000 at its corporate tax rate. If the corporation distributes any funds to Mike, it will be treated as a dividend. Mike will have to pay taxes at the dividend rate. If XYZ, Inc., does not distribute any funds to Mike, then he will not have to pay any taxes on the profits. The value of Mike's interest in the business (i.e., his share price) may rise with the retention of the earnings.

- *Note*: The IRS may challenge corporate accumulated earnings or "reasonable" salaries.

- *Note*: Corporations commonly use schemes to convert shareholder equity into secured or variable-rate debt arrangements. Shareholders will receive interest payments rather than dividends. The corporation can reduce profits by deducting the interest payments, but shareholder generally must include payments as income.

PROFESSIONAL CORPORATIONS

What are professional corporations?

A professional corporation is a type of entity recognized in a limited number of states. It is reserved for service professionals, such as accountants, architects, attorneys, physicians, etc. A professional corporation is afforded limited liability protection, similar to that of a corporation, but is subject to far fewer maintenance requirements and formalities. Shareholders generally hold positions as the only directors and officers in the business. Due to the nature of these entities, eliminating many of these formalities greatly eases the burdens on the shareholders.

- *Note*: Few businesses choose professional corporation status as they are currently taxed at a flat 35% tax rate.

STATUTORY-CLOSE CORPORATIONS

What is a statutory-close corporation?

A statutory-close corporation, as the name implies, is formed pursuant to a special state statute. The business must meet a statutory purpose and other state requirements. Common restrictions include the number of shareholders, classes of stock, and stock restrictions. The primary benefit behind statutory close-corporations is the reduction in corporate formalities.

- *Note*: Many state statutes eliminate the requirement to have a board of directors. Shareholders are allowed to take part in the management and decision making. The shareholders do not have to hold meetings. In general, the governance requirements are similar to those of an LLC.

CHAPTER 10: NON-PROFITS

What is a non-profit?

A non-profit is a business with a mission that qualifies for special tax treatment under the IRC and state revenue codes. The mission must be to undertake a task that the government deems a public necessity or good. A non-profit is generally a corporation, but the corporate entity status is not mandatory.

- *Note*: State statutes often distinguish between non-profits and not-for-profit entities. While these classifications are largely the same, there are some minor differences. Generally, the differences regard membership status and who benefits from the operations of the entity (employees, third-parties or internal members).

What types of activities qualify for non-profit status?

To qualify for Federal, non-profit status, a business' mission must a public purpose, such as charitable, educational, religious, literary purposes, or scientific in nature. There is a lot of room for interpretation within the general categories.

- *Example*: The NCAA college football bowl games are non-profits, but they bring in millions of dollars for the NCAA and the schools involved.

- *Note*: States also recognize business entities as non-profits. State recognition generally depends upon federal recognition of the entity as having a tax exempt (non-profit) purpose. There are many types of activities that qualify for non-profit tax treatment under Section 501(c) of the IRC.

How is a non-profit formed?

Most non-profits are corporations. Unlike a for-profit corporation, non-profit corporations do not issue shares of stock. The corporation chooses to either designate members who vote to elect directors to the corporate board or the incorporate simply appoints the initial board of directors. These directors then govern the business in accordance with the bylaws. This includes the addition or removal of new directors. Some states recognize a specific entity form dedicated to non-profit status. The rules governing these entities facilitate the non-profit mission and add certainty to the maintenance and governance requirements. These are known as non-profit corporations.

To form the non-profit entity, the organizer must undertake the necessary filing requirements with the Secretary of State's office. After receiving an entity charter, the initial board of directors will adopt the organization's bylaws, appoint officers, and complete other organizational requirements. The business must then file for tax exemption with the IRS. The business must complete a Form 1023 packet, which requires specific information about the business' mission, articles, bylaws (or other governance document), capitalization (or expected revenue), the founders (directors), the officers and their compensation, etc. If the business qualifies under IRC Section 501(c), then the IRS will issue a tax exempt certification letter. The business will then follow the required application steps of the State's Department of Revenue (DOR). The DOR will generally require similar information to that required by the IRS in Form 1023, including the IRS exemption letter. Upon approval, the DOR will issue a state income tax exemption letter.

What are the maintenance requirements for non-profits?

The maintenance requirements for a non-profit are similar to those of a corporation. Non-profits must still hold meetings, keep minutes, and maintain other records. One notable difference is that non-profit corporations do not have shareholder's meetings. If the corporation has members, these members may meet in a fashion similar to that of shareholders to take actions within their authority (e.g., vote for directors, approve major corporate actions, etc.). The non-profit must also file annual financial disclosures with the IRS on some variation of Form 990 and with the DOR on the applicable state forms. All records must be available for inspection at its business office or principal place of business.

- *Note*: Failure to file the annual IRS disclosures will result in a revocation of the tax exempt status. States may also require an annual filing with the State's Department of Revenue in order to maintain tax exempt status in that state.

Who owns and controls a non-profit?

Unlike regular corporations, non-profit corporations do not have traditional shareholders or owners. The organizer elects the initial directors, who adopt the bylaws. Since the non-profit is often organized as a corporation, the role of the shareholder becomes synonymous with membership. The original members may be noted in the corporate charter or they may be designated during a board of directors meeting. The board will immediately adopt the bylaws of the corporation. The bylaws determine the procedures for managing and governing the non-profit. The non-profit may have a membership structure where the appointed members vote on the board of directors and on major decisions for the non-profit. In contrast, the non-profit may choose a structure where the board of directors makes all decisions for the non-profit. The members (or the board of directors, depending upon the structure) will vote to elect new directors or to make any major changes to the non-profit. The board will be in charge of hiring officers and establishing compensation structures. The officers will run the daily affairs of the non-profit.

- *Note*: The primary characteristic of a non-profit's control structure is that the directors often taken on the roles assumed by shareholders and directors in a typical corporation.

What is the non-profit continuity?

The non-profit exists independently of its members or directors. If any member or director leaves, the non-profit continues to exist. Since a non-profit does not have owners, there is no need for continuity measures, such as buy-sell agreements. If a non-profit dissolves, it must distribute all of its assets to another non-profit.

- *Note*: Non-profits often have a fixed life. This is common when the non-profit is expected to exhaust a finite endowment of funds. In such a case, once the non-profit has fulfilled its useful purpose then it will dissolve unless the directors take action to extend the life of the entity.

What profit is a non-profit allowed to make?

A non-profit can make a profit on its operations. The limitation is that it cannot return those profits to members or directors of the non-profit. The non-profit must retain any profits and employ those funds in pursuit of its non-profit mission. The profits will be used to pay for the operations and in general support of the non-profit mission. The non-profit may also transfer those funds to other eligible non-profits. The officers in charge of running the non-profit, along with all other employees, may be compensated for their services as in a regular corporation.

- *Example*: Alex founds a non-profit and serves as a board member and president (an officer). The non-profit brings in revenue of $1 million in the year. Alex receives a salary of $200,000 per year for his service as president to the non-profit. Alex, however, cannot receive any portion of the profits outside of his salary. All of the business profits must be reinvested in the businesses operations or transferred to another non-profit.

- *Note*: There are general limitations on the amount of compensation that non-profits can pay to individual employees. There are, however, cases where non-profit CEOs earn over $1 million in annual compensation. As with for-profit corporations, it often depends on whether the regulators find the salary reasonable.

What are the limitations on non-profits?

A non-profit cannot become involved in political campaigns, is limited in its lobbying activity, and cannot distribute profits to any member, director, etc. If the non-profit earns income unrelated to its non-profit purpose, then it must pay income taxes on those profits. Further, the non-profit is limited in the amount of profits that it can receive from the unrelated activities. Unrelated activities are generally subject to normal income tax, as the earnings are not sufficiently related to the non-profit mission.

- *Note*: Excessive unrelated profits can jeopardize the non-profit's tax exempt status with state or federal authorities. Further, a non-profit must benefit a defined class of people and cannot use its funds to benefit one or a small group of people. This is known as the "private benefit" prohibition.

What type of unrelated activities are exempt from taxation?

Several non-profit activities that are not related to the non-profit purpose, but still receive tax exempt treatment are:

- Sales of merchandise that has largely been donated to the non-profit,
- Distributions of items worth less than $5 in return for donations,

- Some activities that primarily benefit members, patients, students, officers or employees of the non-profit,
- Activities where nearly all of the work is done by volunteers, and
- Sales, rentals or exchanges of donor mailing lists.

- *Note*: Engaging in unrelated activities is extremely risky for the non-profit. This generally becomes a concern as the non-profit grows.

What limited liability protection does a non-profit offer?

A non-profit business entity generally has limited personal liability in accordance with its underlying entity status (e.g., a corporation). The directors, officers, and members of a non-profit corporation all receive protection from personal liability for the legal obligations of the non-profit. In certain circumstances, however, limited liability will not provide protection when a director or officer:

- Personally commits a tort,
- Personally guarantees a loan or business debt that is defaulted on by the non-profit,
- Co-mingles personal funds with non-profit funds, or
- Engages in fraudulent or reckless behavior that causes harm.

How does a non-profit raise money?

A primary benefit for a non-profit is that it is eligible for public and private grants and can receive contributions from individuals. If the non-profit is classed for tax purposes as a 501(c)(3), the donation is generally tax deductible for the individual or organization that made the contribution.

- *Example*: GoodGuys, Inc., a local IRC Section 501(c)(3) organization, asks Daniel for a contribution to support the organization. Daniel makes a contribution of $500 to the non-profit. The non-profit can raise money through this type of solicitation. Daniel, in turn, may be able to deduct $500 from his taxable income.

- *Note*: State rules regarding fraud apply when soliciting funds from potential donors to the non-profit. States also often have special rules that non-profits must follow when soliciting its citizens.

What are the main benefits of organizing as a non-profit?

Qualifying organizations pay no tax on federal, state, and local taxes, and therefore can devote a larger proportion of their resources to achieving their particular goals. The status can also qualify groups for special grants or government funding, as well as special rates for services or even postage. Donors prefer making contributions to these groups because they can generally deduct the payments from their own taxes. Non-profits are exempt from local property tax. The form of the organization offers advantages in itself. Since non-profits may exist as corporations, they may also possess all the benefits of corporate status. As previously discussed, the corporate form shields owners and managers of the organization from personal liability for the group's actions, subject to certain legal exceptions. Non-profit incorporation also serves a strategic goal by formalizing the group's goals and helps maintain organizational focus as the effort grows.

- *Note*: The benefits of non-profit status should accrue to the business and its operations. These benefits should generally not accrue to individual members of the non-profit.

What are the disadvantages of organizing as a non-profit?

Despite the advantages noted above, non-profit status has numerous disadvantages. Drawbacks to the status include:

- Inability to divide profits among members;
- Limitations on the sources of the group's income; and
- Restrictions on the use of assets to tax exempt purposes expressed in the governing documents.

CHAPTER 11: IDENTIFYING THE APPROPRIATE STARTUP ENTITY

THE SOLE PROPRIETORSHIP

What are the primary considerations in carrying on business as a sole proprietorship?

If the entrepreneur is the sole owner of the business activity, the ease of formation and flexibility of the entity make a sole proprietorship a very easy and convenient form of business entity. The major concern for the sole proprietor is personal liability for the debts of the business. There are some situations, however, where forming a business entity with limited liability protection does nothing to protect the individual owner.

- *Note:* If an entrepreneur provides a service, does not have employees, and does not have a physical space open to clients, then a sole proprietorship may be an appropriate entity form.

- *Example*: Tom is a freelance consultant who does any work on the contracting employer's work sight. He strictly provides personal services. He does not sell any products, have a place of business, or employ any employees. In such a case, a sole proprietorship may be appropriate for Tom's business.

Is a sole proprietorship ever appropriate for a business that sells products?

If the entrepreneur produces or sells a product, then a customer could potentially be harmed (physically or financially) by the product. This could lead to liability for the defective design or manufacture of the product. For this reason, a limited liability entity is generally the best choice for product businesses. In contrast, this is not a concern for a service provider. While a service provider may commit malpractice for a client, a limited liability entity will not protect her. Remember, an individual is always personally liable for her own activity. Forming a limited liability entity would not shield her.

- *Example*: Winston is a mechanical engineer and designer. He enters a work-for-hire agreement to design and build a machine that will construct a certain type of toy for Toy Company, Inc. Winston is compensated primarily for his design service and also receives compensation when his employee (a machinist) constructs the final product. The product later malfunctions and injures several Toy Company employees. The employees receive worker's compensation from Toy Company but now wish to sue Winston for product liability. If Winston is a sole proprietor, he will be personally liable for the injuries. A limited liability entity may protect Winston from personal liability if his employee improperly manufactured the product. It may not protect him if his design was defective as he personally designed the product.

- *Note*: Product liability is a strict liability tort. A plaintiff would not have to show that a manufacturer is negligent in any way. If the good is used in a reasonably foreseeable manner and it harms the user, then the manufacturer or seller of the good can be held liable.

Is a sole proprietorship appropriate for a business that has employees?

The analysis changes if our sole proprietor in the above scenario is an employer. As previously stated, she will be liable for her own malpractice and a limited liability entity will not protect her personal assets. If she has employees, however, a limited liability entity could afford her a layer of protection. As a sole proprietor, any employee of the business acts as her agent. As discussed in chapter 3, these agents could potentially cause her personal liability in contract or tort. A limited liability entity will protect her from personal liability for the actions of agents (employees). The actions of the employees will subject the business entity to liability and not the owner.

- *Example*: Janice is an attorney who provides estate planning services to clients. She employs Eric as a secretary. Janice and Eric routinely receive lots of personal information about clients, including private health information. Eric learns that a client has a likely fatal disease and he discloses that information to his friends. If the client is adversely affected by the disclosure of this private health information, they may have a cause of action against Eric and Janice's law firm for disclosing the information (e.g., an invasion of privacy claim). If Janice is a sole proprietor, Eric's actions could subject her to personal liability.

- *Note*: If the owner chooses a limited liability entity status to protect herself from personal liability for the act of agent, she will still have to maintain business formalities for the business entity to avoid being disregarded by the court.

Should a business with a physical business location that is open to the public operate as a sole proprietorship?

A business that opens its doors to the public risks personal liability for injuries suffered by customers or clients entering the premises. The business owner has a duty to keep the premises reasonably safe for the public. If she drops below this standard, then she could be held liable for her negligence. A limited liability entity status does not protect the entity from liability, but it will protect the owner from personal liability for the business' negligence in a case like this.

- *Example*: Alice has a photography business. She invites individuals into her photo studio to take portraits. Her equipment is all electronic and she runs electrical cords across the floor to power the equipment. A family comes into the studio to take a family portrait, and the mother trips on the cord and injures herself. In a sole proprietorship Alice would be personally liable for negligently failing to warn customers about the cords or failing to secure the cords in a manner to reduce the possibility of injury.

- *Note*: Common examples of failure to keep the premises safe include slip-and-fall accidents. If the owner knows that the floor is slippery (or should know that the floor is slippery) and fails to warn patrons, then she has fallen below her duty of care. A limited liability entity could create a layer of protection for the owner. A slip-and-fall accident would subject the business entity to liability, but would shield the owner's personal assets.

Should a business with potential contract liability operate as a sole proprietorship?

Lastly, a sole proprietor is personally liable on any contracts of the business. A contract is any transactional arrangement, whether or not reduced to writing, including any business loans or other payment obligations. It also includes any loans, contracts, or other obligations that are in the business's name. Even if the business provides services and does not have a place of business, or employees, then it still may be advantageous to adopt a limited liability entity form. The limited liability entity status will shield the business owner's personal assets from attachment by creditors in the event of contractual loss (such as a breach of contract).

- *Example*: Gary is a sole proprietor. As part of his business, he enters into multiple contracts with suppliers and distributors. If Gary's business is unable to perform its contract obligations or otherwise breaches these contracts, Gary will be personally liable for any damages arising pursuant to the breach.

- *Note*: Choosing a limited liability form to shield the sole proprietor from personal liability on contracts may not advance the interests of the business. In reality it is unlikely any lender will lend to this type of limited liability entity and not require a personal guarantee from the owner. Larger, more established businesses have assets sufficient to securitize business debts. Smaller businesses often lack these assets. Lenders will not take the risk of loss associated with lending to these businesses without a personal guarantee by the owner.

PARTNERSHIPS

What are the primary considerations for the GP?

When multiple individuals establish a business venture, a GP offers numerous advantages. The GP form allows for flexibility in operations and governance. The parties can allocate ownership, profits and losses, and authority in any way they desire. Further, the GP provides pass-through taxation to the partners. This avoids the double taxation associated with corporate entity forms and may result in a lower tax burden on the employer. The benefits and detriments of the pass-through tax structure are discussed below in the context of the LLC. Taken together, these characteristics make the GP seem a viable entity type for a startup.

- *Note*: Many of the characteristics of the sole proprietorship apply equally to the GP. The notable distinction of the GP is that it involves two or more persons as partners. Each partner is an agent of the business in the same way that an employee is an agent. This leads to concerns over agency liability for the partners.

A GP, however, is perhaps the most risky form of business entity. As with the sole proprietorship, the partner is personally liable for all debts and torts of the business. The GP magnifies this risk, as each partner is also personally liable for the tortious actions of each partner. Recall the discussion from Chapter 3 on tort liability for the agents of the business. Each partner is also an agent of the business for purposes of contracting and has authority to carry out any acts on behalf of the GP because of these risks. A GP should only be considered when a limited liability entity would not provide protection to the parties.

- *Note*: A GP between a marital couple in a community property state may be appropriate if: it is a service partnership, does not have a business location open to the public, and there are no other employees. The reason is because the jointly held or owned assets of the couple may already be at risk by the actions of either spouse. As such, an alternative entity form will not protect those assets.

What are the primary considerations for the LP?

If the sole proprietor from the earlier example needs investment capital for her business, a LP may be appropriate. LPs have all of the flexibility in entity governance and maintenance associated with a GP, but also provide limited liability to its limited partners. The limited partner has no liability for business debts or liability above her capital investment. That is, she cannot lose more money that she has invested in the business. This status is similar within any limited liability entity. The general partner(s), on the other hand, have no personal liability protection. They will still be liable as general partners for any debts or liabilities of the business.

- *Note*: LPs are generally not used in startup ventures. The LP form exposes the general partner to a great deal of personal liability for the business activities. LPs are primarily used in specialty industries where one or more limited liability entities serve as the general partner(s). Most venture capital and private equity funds are organized as LPs.

What are the considerations for a LLP?

LLPs are a valid form of entity for professional service providers. In fact, most state laws restrict these entities to these types of organizations. The benefit of this type of entity is that it allows for the flexibility of a GP and for the limited personal liability of the partners.

- *Note*: State law sometimes limits liability protection by protecting partners from liability for tortious activity of other partners or employees but making partners personally liable for the contractual debts of the business.

LIMITED LIABILITY COMPANIES

What are the primary considerations for the LLC?

A LLC is likely the most popular and fastest growing entity choice for small businesses in the

United States. For startup businesses, the LLC combines the favorable attributes of a GP with those of the corporation. Notably, the LLC entity form can have any number of members, it offers a high level of flexibility in management and governance, and provides pass-through taxation to the members. Perhaps most importantly, it provides limited liability to the managers. These attributes are the reason that the LLC is such a popular entity form.

- *Note*: As a newer entity form, state law has not fully developed around the LLC. Many states have adopted model LLC acts to provide an additional level of certainty in the law surrounding the LLC.

How does the LLC management structure provide benefits for a startup?

A key benefit to the startup LLC is the ability to customize the management structure. Recall that the LLC offers two types of management organization, member-managed and manager-managed. The member-managed LLC is very similar to a GP in that each member has the authority to act on behalf of the business. This entity form allows the LLC to avoid withholding payroll taxes (a significant administrative burden), as the members often pay self-employment taxes on their distributions. If, however, any of the members do not wish to take part in daily affairs of the business or wish to hire professional managers, the LLC allows for this as well. In such a situation, the non-managing members will act more like the shareholders and board of directors in a corporation. They will vote and collaborate on major decisions, but the daily operation of the LLC is left to the managers. Combine this flexibility in structure with limited liability protection for each member, and the LLC is a superior form of entity for many small businesses.

- *Note*: Generally, an LLC will withhold payroll taxes on salaried employees of the business. If, however, members are selected as managers to run the business and receive a salary, this salary will be treated as a guaranteed payment to the member. The LLC will not withhold payroll taxes from the member's payment; rather, the employee will report the guaranteed salary as self-employment income.

What are the primary drawbacks to using an LLC as a startup structure?

The primary drawback to an LLC as a startup structure is the lack of formalized procedures for selling an ownership interest to outside investors. Corporations have a developed entity structure and a well-defined body of law surrounding shareholder rights. LLCs are a much newer form of entity and, by default, have only one class of equity ownership — the membership unit. Many state statutes, however, allow for multiple classes of membership unit, as investors generally desire a preferred class of security. If the LLC wants to create classes of voting member with rights and authority similar to that of common and preferred shareholders in a corporation, it has to do so through a combination of provisions in the operating agreement and contractual agreements among the members. Drafting these contracts can be more complex and expensive than in a corporation, as LLC law is less developed in many states and may require greater effort by the legal practitioners. Further, each time there is a change in membership or growth in the business, these contracts may need to be updated. If the LLC needs this level of structural sophistication, the cost and difficulty of creation and maintenance may far exceed that of a corporate entity form. Further, equity investors are often reluctant to invest in LLCs. The lack of certainty in the entity form, a lack of understanding of the multiple classes of ownership interest, and the burden of maintenance dissuade investors from investing in the entity.

- *Note*: Adopting the LLC to meet the growth needs of a startup venture is often difficult. To mimic the provisions of preferred shares in a corporation, the LLC may be forced to issue contractually restricted membership units that vest over a period of time. The LLC will have to create special agreements for granting options to employees. The LLC does not have authorized shares, so any new distribution of equity requires the authorization of new membership units. Outside investors often want preferred status with regard to distributions, voting rights, liquidation preferences, etc. Arranging for all of these special arrangements in an LLC is difficult and is very likely to produce conflicts among owners.

When is a LLC tax structure advantageous for startups?

LLCs are generally only appropriate for startup ventures when the founders use the entity to take advantage of the pass-through taxation features. Benefits associated with pass-through taxation that are common to partnerships and LLCs are as follows:

- *Pass-Through Taxation* - Profits are easily withdrawn from the business entity without additional tax consequences.

- *Special Allocations* - Investors may designate special allocations of LLC profits and losses in a given year that do not correspond exactly with the ownership structure.

- *Passive Income* - Profit may be designated as passive income in certain scenarios.

- *Basis Adjustment* - The ability to adjust an owner's basis (outside basis) in the entity can give rise to certain tax benefits.

- *Inside Basis* - The internal basis (inside basis) in property contributed to the entity can give rise to certain tax benefits.

- *Profits Interest* - The LLC allows members to receive a profits-only interest stake in the venture that avoids some of the tax implications of purchasing equity in the venture. Such flexibility is not available in a corporate form.

What are the tax disadvantages for a startup to file as an LLC?

While the LLC offers pass-through taxation to owners, there are numerous tax disadvantages. Many of the specialty provisions that an LLC may introduce do not receive the tax advantages that corporate securities receive. For example, LLC shares may not qualify for the benefits associated with Qualified Small Business Stock under IRC Section 1045. The primary tax concerns of the LLC as a startup entity are as follows:

- *Active Income* - LLC income or losses may be treated as "active" income.

- *Self-Employment Taxes* - LLC members' income allocation may be subject to self-employment tax.

- *Phantom Income* - LLC profits or sweat-equity arrangements can give rise to phantom income, as discussed in Chapters 4 & 6.

- *Ordinary Income Property* - A member who contributes assets to the business that are considered "Ordinary Income Assets" (see IRC Section 751) can give rise to ordinary income for the contributing member.

CORPORATIONS

What are the primary considerations for startups considering a corporate entity status?

Corporations provide numerous advantages to a startup business. A benefit is the ability to customize the management structure to meet the needs of the entrepreneur(s) and the outside investors. The corporation offers the greatest degree of personal liability protection for owners in their roles as shareholder, director, or officer. It also allows flexibility in providing employees with equity incentives, such as vesting plans and option plans. There is also a litany of tax-associated benefits both for C and S corporations.

What about the C corporation maintenance requirements?

The corporate entity form provides a comprehensive business structure, limited liability for employees, and the ability to sell and distribute shares to equity investors. There are two primary concerns when selecting C corporation status: entity governance requirements and the double taxation of business profits. In general, the corporate form requires far more formal maintenance procedures than other entity forms. These requirements are discussed in greater detail in Chapter 9.

What are the benefits and detriments of the double tax structure?

The double taxation structure will often lead to higher tax liability for owners of the corporation than in a pass-through taxation entity. There are scenarios, however, where the double taxation of corporate profits will yield a lower total tax burden on owners. This is possible because of the ever-changing taxation rates and the responsibility of individuals to pay self-employment taxes on certain pass-through income.

- *Note*: The individual and corporate taxes rate changes from year to year. In any given year a combination of the corporate tax rate and the individual dividend rate may be lower than the taxpayer's individual income tax rate. This is particularly true when you include responsibility for payroll or self-employment taxes, which are not included in dividend payments.

- *Example*: Derek is the sole owner of a C corporation. The corporation earns profits of $10,000 in a year. The corporation will pay taxes on the income at its corporate tax rate. We will use 25% for purposes of this example. This leave $7,500 in profit. Now, when this $7,500 is distributed to Derek, he will pay taxes on the dividend at the applicable dividend rate. We will use 20% for purposes of this example. After taxes, Derek will receive $6,000 of the after-tax profits of the corporation. If the business were a pass-through entity, such as an LLC, Eric may be subject to self-employment taxes on the profits, as well as personal income taxes. If his personal income tax rate is 36%, and his total self-employment tax liability is 15.8%, then he would receive $5,820 in after-tax profits of the LLC.

One advantage to the double taxation regime is the ability to retain profits (and in some cases losses) at the corporate level. As is the case in startups, if the investors wish to reinvest profits, the C corporation avoids the issue of "phantom income". As previously discussed, phantom income arise when a business owner is taxed on her share of business profits when there is no distribution. The disadvantage of this scenario is that business losses are not passed through to shareholders; rather, the corporation retains these loses. These losses are generally available to offset income from the past 2 years and for the next 20 years. In the event of a merger or sale of the corporation, these losses can be valuable to the acquiring entity.

- *Example*: Tom owns a C corporation. It makes a profit at the end of the year of $30,000. The corporation will have to pay income taxes on that $30,000 at the applicable corporate tax rate. If the business does not distribute any of the profits to Tom, then he does not pay taxes on those funds. If the business were organized as a LLC or S corporation, then Tom would have to pay taxes on the profits attributable to him as owner. In other words, the C corporation entity form avoids the "phantom income" situation.

- *Note*: Accumulated losses are not lost in a startup that seeks to benefit investors and owners at the time of business exit. Any losses retained by the corporation at the time of an exit event (e.g., sale of the business) can be used to offset any capital gains taxes incurred by the owners/investors at the time of sale. Congress has also enacted special rules to benefit small business owners operating in the corporate form.

What other tax benefits exist for the C corporation?

A detailed description of the tax benefits associated with any business entity are beyond the scope of this text; however, it is important that you have a general understanding of the primary tax benefits available for startup ventures. Below is a list and short description of many of the tax-associated, C corporation benefits for further research.

- *Shareholder and Employee Benefits* - The corporation can provide to shareholders and employees certain health, welfare and retirement benefits that are tax deductible to the corporation.

- *Fiscal Year Election* - The corporation has greater flexibility in designating a fiscal year other than the calendar year.

- *Long-Term Capital Gain Rates* - Gains on the sale of stock of a C corporation held by a shareholder for more than one year are taxed at a 15% tax rate. This is often far lower than the tax rate for individual income.

- *Ordinary Loss Treatment* - IRC Section 1244 allows the shareholder of a qualifying C corporation to treat any losses on the sale of the corporation's stock as an ordinary loss up to $50K for individuals or $100K for married couples per year. This means that the losses can offset ordinary income. Generally, such losses are treated as capital losses and can only be used to offset capital gains. To qualify, the C corporation cannot have a market capitalization (contributions and retained earnings) greater than $1 million, and the shareholder must be the original purchaser of the loss-producing shares sold. This means that shares awarded for services rendered to the corporation are not eligible for the ordinary loss treatment.

- *Qualified Small Business Stock Benefits*

  - IRC Section 1045 allows individual shareholders to defer the recognition of any gain on the sale of qualified small business stock (QSBS). The requirements to qualify as QSBS are extensive. The corporation must have less than $50M in gross assets at the time of issuance; the issuance must take place after Aug 10, 1993; the shares must be acquired by the original issuee; and the shares must held by a non-corporate taxpayer. For a transaction to qualify, the shareholder must have held the stock for longer than six months. Further, the proceeds from sale must be reinvested in another qualified small business within 60 days of the date of sale. Deferring the recognition of any gain on sale can be very attractive for startup owners.

  - IRC Section 1202 allows shareholders to exclude from income up to 50% of the gain on the sale of the QSBS up to $10 million or ten times the shareholder's basis in the stock, whichever is greater. There are, however, significant limits on this provision. This provision applies to QSBS issued directly to C corporation shareholders after Aug. 10, 1993. The exclusion is not available to shareholders who are not the original issuee and the C corporation cannot have more than $50 million in assets at the time the stock is issued. The downside to this provision is that the 50% of the gain that is recognized is taxable at a flat 28%, which is well higher than the current 15% long-term capital gain rate.

What other tax detriments exist for the C corporation?

The primary tax detriment for C corporations, discussed at length throughout this text, is the double taxation structure. Much time is spent in corporate tax planning to avoid the negative consequences that exist in this structure. Below are a few of the major tax detriments associated with the C corporation:

- *Corporate Losses* - The shareholder of a corporation cannot use or otherwise take advantage of corporate losses. In an S corporation, the entity losses flow through to the taxpayer. This is not the case in the C corporation. Losses are trapped at the entity level and can generally be used to offset profit in the previous 2 years or in the following 20 years.

- *Fixed Corporate Basis* - Startups organized as C corporations often distribute stock to shareholders in exchange for value to the corporation. The value of services, cash, guarantees of debt, or property provided to the corporation in exchange for the stock is the shareholder's basis in that stock. The shareholder's basis in that stock remains fixed and does not vary with the performance of the corporation, as is the case with other entities. The ability to adjust one's basis can be a significant advantage for the shareholder, but this action is not available in the C corporation without additional contribution of capital.

- *Capital Gain Rates* - Capital gains on the sale of property held by a C corporation are taxed at the corporation's ordinary income tax rate. In a flow-through entity, however, owners enjoy a lower personal capital gain rate on the sale of property by the entity.

- *Redemption of Stock for Cash* - If a C corporation redeems (repurchases) the stock of a shareholder, then the entire purchase price is treated as a dividend to the shareholder to the extent of the corporations earnings and profits. Currently, dividend and capital gain rates are equal. The issue, however, is that the shareholder's basis is not recovered prior to treating the distribution as a dividend. The shareholder may be forced to claim a capital loss on the transfer of the stock back to the corporation. There is, however, an exemption to this rule under IRC Section 302(b). This provision allows the shareholder to treat the redemption as a sale of the shares to the corporation if certain requirements are met. As such, upon redemption, the shareholder recovers her basis in the shares before incurring a tax liability for the gains or losses incurred. When considering redemption of C corporation stock, consult a professional to plan for a redemption scenario with the lowest possible tax repercussions.

- *Redemption of Stock for Property* - The above scenario demonstrates a negative tax consequence when a corporation redeems the equity of a shareholder for cash. Another issue arises when the corporation redeems those shares for property in the corporation. If the property has a built-in gain then the distribution will cause a gain tax to the corporation and a dividend to the shareholder for the fair market value of the property. As is the case above, the corporation can avoid this tax consequence if an IRC Section 302(b) exception applies.

- *Excess Accumulated Earnings* - IRC Section 531 allows for a tax penalty on C corporations that retain excessive earnings, rather than distributing those earnings to shareholders. A corporation must show a reasonable business need for retaining such earnings to avoid a

20% corporate tax penalty on those earnings. This situation is generally not a concern for startups, as most startups readily employ their earnings in growing the business and have a reasonable business need for retaining earnings.

- *Alternative Minimum Tax (AMT)* - Corporations are subject to the AMT. This is a complicated calculation that makes certain that corporation pay income tax on a minimum percentage of attributed income in a given year. It seeks to avoid the effects of excessive deductions, credits, and other tax deferral arrangements on the corporation's income tax liability in a given year. There are numerous exemptions for new corporation with less than $5M in gross receipts within the first 5 years of operations and less than $7.5M in gross receipts in any 3 years of operations. The AMT is normally not a threat for startup ventures that often incur extensive losses during the development stages.

How does the C corporation equity structure benefit the startup?

Lastly, and probably the greatest advantage for entrepreneurs, the C corporation allows for the authorization and distribution of multiple classes of stock. While founders of a corporation receive common stock, equity investors generally require preferred stock interests. Preferred equity provides the investors with various levels of protection from loss, such as a dividend preference, liquidation preference, participation rights, redemption rights, etc.

- *Note*: The preferences generally regard the right to recover one's invested capital before any other equity owners receive any proceeds of an exit (known as a "liquidation preference"). The details of preferred stock and terms of investment are complicated subjects that exceed the scope of this text.

What about the S corporation?

An S corporation provides the organizational structure of a corporation and pass-through taxation similar to that of a partnership (with several notable differences). The difficulty for many startups in choosing S corporation entity status is that the business activity must meet numerous requirements in order to qualify for the election. Recall, there can be no more than 100 investors, each must be an individual, an American citizen (or resident alien), and there can only be one class of equity ownership. All of these factors are of primary concern to growth-based startups.

- *Note*: Remember that the startup venture is growth-based. It depends upon outside capital from investors to achieve its growth targets. Many outside investors, such as venture capital firms, are businesses. An S corp does not allow these business entities to own an equity interest in the business. Further, outside investors generally purchase a preferred class of business ownership. The S corp does not allow for the designation of a preferred or special class of ownership. Each of these issues is discussed below.

What tax benefits exist for the S corporation?

The primary benefit of an S corporation is pass-through taxation. That is, the business entity does not pay taxes; rather, the income or losses of the business activity pass through the business entity and are reported on the income tax returns of the individual owners. In this regard, the S corporation enjoys the structural characteristics of a C corporation with a tax structure very similar to that of partnership and LLCs. Other beneficial income tax characteristics of the S corporation are as follows:

- *Passive Income* - Owners of an S corporation treat business profits as passive income. Owners working in the S corporation must receive a salary for services rendered to the business. This salary is subject to payroll taxes for the employer and employee. Passive income for shareholders who are not "material participants" in the organization is subject to ordinary income tax rates, but is not subject to payroll taxes by the business or the employee.

- *Basis Adjustments* - Like a partnership-taxed entity, the S corporation shareholder's basis is adjusted up or down by earnings and distributions of the business. The individual shareholder pays income taxes on her share of the S corporation profit. If the S corporation retains (does not distribute) any profits, the shareholders' basis in the business increase by this amount.

What tax detriments exist for the S corporation?

The primary tax detriment of the S corporation is the counter to the advantages of the S corporation tax structure. That is, losses that pass through the S corporation to shareholders who do not "materially participate" in S corporation activities are passive losses. Passive losses can only be used to offset passive income. Another common tax detriment is the inability to make special allocations in the S corporation. That is, shareholders receive a percentage of business profits and losses based upon their respective ownership interests in the entity. In contrast, partnership-taxed entities are able to make special allocations to shareholders and C corporations are able to issue preferred stock that may alter the distribution of business profits or losses.

How does the S corporation compare to the LLC as a startup entity?

The 100 investor limitation is not a primary area of concern between an LLC and S corporation, as most startups do not achieve this mark before going through extensive equity offerings. Both entities provide similar flow-through structures for taxation. If the startup requires adherence to the corporate entity structure (shareholders, directors, and officers) then the S corporation avoids the burdens of establishing these roles through contractual arrangement.

The first major drawback of the S corporation is the limitation to one class of equity security. The S corporation, unlike the LLC, does not allow for profit-only interest stakes in the venture. This type of interest may be considered a security and disqualify the entity from S corporation status.

- *Example*: Alfred is an angel investor. He identifies Morgan's startup as a promising venture. Morgan is currently organized as an S corporation. Alfred is not interested in common stock in the S corporation. He wants to make certain that when the business is sold in the future that he will receive a return on his investment before Morgan or anyone else receives any of the proceeds. As such, he asks that Morgan convert the entity into a C corporation. She can then authorize a second class of preferred stock that has a liquidation preference. When Alfred invests in the business, he will receive preferred stock in exchange for his invested capital.

- *Note*: Recall, preferred shares allow a special allocation of interest (dividend, liquidation preference, decision rights, etc.) that are not available to the common stock holder. S corporations and LLCs cannot issue preferred stock, but the LLC can issue alternative interests that are not available to the S corporation. The profit-only interest is a common LLC right given to outside investors who seek special rights.

A second drawback is that the S corporation does not allow for special allocations of profits and losses. Each shareholder must share in the income in direct proportion to their ownership interest.

- *Example*: Bob, Kate, and Julie form an S corporation for their business and each hold the same number of shares in the business. Bob works in the business part-time, Kate works full time and Julie is just a silent investor. Bob and Kate will receive a salary for their work in the business. After that, all profits of the corporation are distributed equally to the owners. All three shareholders realize that the business is successful based largely on the efforts of Bob. They determine that Bob should receive more of the business profits that Kate and Julie. They are disappointed to learn that they cannot make a special allocation of profits to Bob that is different from his ownership percentage. If they were an LLC, then they could make this special allocation. They decide to pay Bob an additional bonus as part of his salary rather than an additional allocation of business profits.

- *Note*: Most startup investors do not wish to receive a distribution from the business activity. The money is better reinvested to grow the business. These businesses will, however, seek to use an allocation of losses to offset other income. The ability to specifically allocate income or loss could be an important draw to an outside investor.

A third important distinction between the LLC and S corporation is how business profits are taxed to the owners. In an LLC the members pay ordinary income taxes (possibly including self-employment taxes) on their distributions received from LLC profits. This result is largely the same whether the LLC is member-managed or manager-managed. In an S corporation, employee-shareholders receive a salary for their services to the business. They also receive a distribution of business profits based upon their percentage of ownership. These employees pay ordinary income and self-employment taxes on their salary. They also pay ordinary income taxes on their distributive share of profits. While employee shareholders pay self-employment taxes on their salaries, S corporations shareholders who are passive investors do not pay self-employment taxes on their distributive share.

- *Example*: In the above example, Bob receives both salary and a distribution of profits from the S corporation. His salary will be subject to payroll taxes. He will pay a portion of those taxes and the business will pay the other portion. His share of S corporation profits, however, is treated as passive income. He will be subject to income tax on his share of income but will not have to pay self-employment taxes on that amount.

- *Note*: The fact that passive investors in the S corporation (or any corporation for that matter) do not pay self-employment taxes on their share of income is a huge advantage to those investors (such as angel investors and venture capitalists). This fact alone leads many investors to prefer the S corporation status over the LLC. The IRS has considered aligning the taxation of distributions to members of a member-managed LLC with those of passive investors in an S corporation. The recommendations were made more than a decade ago, but Congress has not yet acted on the recommendations.

Another disadvantage is that funds guaranteed on behalf of the S corp are not part of the basis or at-risk amount of shareholders. This means that personally guaranteeing a business loan does not provide the tax advantages available to the partnership or LLC. If a business expects to incur extensive losses in a given year, then investors may seek to use these losses to offset their other income. Rather than invest all of the money employed by the business, many investors/owners will personally guarantee third-party loans to the business. In a partnership (and LLC) these loans raise the investor's basis in the business, so that sustained losses can be used in excess of the actual capital invested. An S corp does not allow an increase in basis for personally guaranteed loans. As such, some of the losses incurred in the business may not be useable by the investors due to basis limitations. Lending money directly to the corporation, however, will help the shareholder in using the losses by increasing her "debt basis".

- *Note*: The inability to increase one's basis by personally guaranteeing loans is not a large concern for outside investors. Angel and institutional investors do not frequently guarantee loans; rather, they infuse cash whenever needed.

Lastly, and perhaps the most important limitation for startups in choosing an S corporation entity status, is the requirement that all members be individuals (not businesses). Venture capital firms are organized as LPs, with an LLC or corporation serving as general partner in the relationship. The LP will invest funds by purchasing equity in the business entity. This arrangement effectively prohibits venture capital investment in businesses organized as S corporations.

- *Note*: This may not be an issue for early stage startups who seek angel investment. Angel investors are high-net-worth individuals who invest (much in the same way as venture capital firms) in startup ventures. These individuals may be willing to invest in S corporations, and they do not run afoul of the individual investor requirement.

What about a non-profit entity?

A startup generally cannot operate as a non-profit due to the inability to have owners (investors). While some businesses organize and grow large in non-profit status, it is generally in select industries, such as medicine and literary publications.

- *Note*: Non-profits do not allow earnings to inure to owners. The only funds available to members of a non-profit are salaries paid for services rendered. While such salaries may be very lucrative, there are certain IRS limitations on the amount an employee of a non-profit is allowed to receive as compensation.

CHAPTER 12: SETTING UP THE BUSINESS ENTITY

The previous chapters discuss the primary considerations in selecting the appropriate business entity. Once the decision is made, properly setting up a business entity requires a great deal of effort. Below we provide the primary steps involved in setting up the entity and preparing it to accomplish the startup's objectives.

- *Note*: Recall that a sole proprietorship and partnership may arise by the default actions of the business owner(s). This section refers to the process of registering an entity with the state and preparing the organizational governance documents.

What goes into the entity formation process?

Contrary to popular belief, the entity formation process can be somewhat complicated. Many people believe entity formation to be easy because the actual filing and receipt of the formation documents is a simple process. However, as discussed in previous chapters, there is much more that goes into setting up a business entity effectively. That is, setting up the entity so that it is customized to meet the needs of the business. The following paragraphs give a step-by-step overview of the things that need to be either done or considered when forming the entity.

What do I file with the state Secretary of State's Office?

First, the organizer (or incorporator) will visit the Secretary of State's webpage and verify the availability of the intended business name. If the name is available and she is not going to immediately file all of the necessary documents, she will want to reserve the name. This will prevent others from taking the name in the interim. Next she must file the application for formation (the articles of incorporation or articles of organization). Most state's have an electronic system to prepare the application that takes the organizer through some simple steps. While this is a simple manner of creating the organizational documents, it is often advisable to add company specific provisions (such as restrictions on the right to amend the articles). The organizer can always prepare her own articles and upload it through the electronic system.

What tax documents do I file?

During the filing process, the incorporator will prepare and file Form SS-4 (Application for Employer Identification Number) with the IRS and also apply for a state tax reporting number. If the business sells goods, it may also be necessary to apply for a state sales tax number. Later, the incorporator or an appointed officer will undertake to set up deposit or withholding accounts for employee income and payroll taxes. Luckily, numerous software products make it easy to withhold these taxes and report and deposit them with the appropriate taxing authority.

When do I draft the entity governance documents?

Any time before or during this process, the organizer should begin preparing the partnership agreement, operating agreement, or bylaws. Drafting these documents requires a great deal of work and consideration regarding the business operations. The documents will govern nearly every aspect of the business operations including: decision-making; authority or voting rights of owners; composition of the board; etc. The provisions typically included in the governance documents are numerous and can be complex. A great deal of business strategy and ethos goes into these documents. For this reason, the organizer should work with all of the founders to address the governance provisions. It is also advisable to consult an attorney in drafting these provisions.

What actions do the organizers of a partnership take?

Recall from Chapters 6 & 7 that GPs arise by default, while LPs and LLPs must be filed with the state. The formation of the partnership, however, is only one aspect of setting up the business entity. The next step is for the individual partners to enter into a detailed partnership agreement outlining the rights, authority, ownership, and liability of the individual partners. Each partner must sign the agreement for it to be effective against that partner. The partnership may also ratify and agree to hold the organizer harmless for any activity in establishing the partnership.

What actions do the organizers of the LLC take?

Organizers of a LLC must undertake procedures similar to that of a partnership that files with the state. The LLC is not required to have formal meetings, but the members should act quickly to adopt an operating agreement. Like the partnership agreement, the operating agreement should cover all of the important structural, financial, and operational aspects of the business. The LLC may also ratify or agree to hold the organizer harmless for activities undertaken in forming the LLC.

What actions do the incorporators and initial board of directors of a corporation take?

The Secretary of State's Office will review the application for incorporation and either accept or reject the application. If the application is rejected, the department will indicate the deficiency in the application and allow amendment. Once the corporate charter is issued, the corporation now exists. Now the incorporator has to take steps to set up the corporate structure. The first step is to call a corporate meeting. In this meeting the incorporator will appoint the initial directors and the corporate secretary. The corporate secretary will record this action in the minutes and may prepare a resolution for the incorporator. At this point the board of directors has authority. The board prepares and signs the "Actions of Incorporator", which adopts or ratifies all previous actions taken by the incorporator and relieves her from her responsibilities. Next the board will approve all expenses associated with formation, including any funds paid to the incorporator. Now the board of directors must take numerous actions to completely setup the entity structure.

The next task for the board of directors is to adopt the corporate bylaws. This is done by identifying the bylaws in the initial meeting and voting on their acceptance. Again the corporate secretary may prepare a resolution for the board's signature. At this point the board will proceed with the meeting in accordance with the rules for director meetings as laid out in the bylaws. The board will then address the following tasks in any given order:

- Authorizing the principal office or place of business;

- Preparing and filing of qualification to do business as a foreign corporation in any other states;

- Designating the corporate fiscal year;

- Ratifying the corporate Employer Identification Number;

- Designating the size of the board of directors (which is generally included in the bylaws);

- Undertaking the election of officers;

- Designating of management powers as appropriate;

- Authorization of corporate stock (number of shares and classes of shares if there are multiple classes);

- Approving the issuance of founder's stock (common stock) to the business founders;

- Approving any stock option grants to founders (if applicable);

- Approving the minutes,

- Authorizing the corporate seal and stock certificates;

- Approving the subchapter "S" tax election for the corporation (if applicable);

- Authorizing the management to open bank accounts;

- Approving any proprietary information and inventions agreements;

- Approving any indemnification agreements with officers and directors;

- Approving any stock option or issuance plans or option agreements'

Many of the actions of the board are authorized in the articles of incorporation and bylaws. The board can only act within the bounds of these governing documents.

What actions do the shareholders of the corporation take?

The initial meeting will generally conclude by a call for the shareholders (i.e., founders) to vote to formally elect the board of directors. Remember, the initial board of directors was appointed by the incorporator. It is important to have the newly minted shareholders to follow the bylaws and formally elect the standing members of the board. Generally, the shareholders will also vote for secondary tasks, such as approving the indemnification agreement for officers and directors and approving the stock option or issuance plans.

- *Note*: Many of these actions (by directors or shareholders) may be taken outside of a formal meeting through signed consents. When this happens the consents must generally be unanimous, unless the bylaws expressly indicate otherwise. Corporate formalities require that the company maintain records of all corporate meetings, resolutions, stock issuances, and initial capitalization data. Most corporations use commercial software to track this information.

What formal steps should the corporate board take with regard to issuing corporate equity?

During the initial meeting, the board of directors generally issues "Founders' Restricted Stock" to the company founders. This is a form of common stock that is expressly restricted from resale by the founders. The issuance is done through purchase agreements or subscription agreements. The purchase agreement may contain standard terms by which the stock vests in the founders over a period of time (i.e., the restrictions will lapse a little each year). When issuing equity, the corporation should prepare the following documents:

- Stock Certificates and Receipts for the receiving founders,
- Memoranda memorializing the IRC Section 83(b) tax elections of each founder (discussed further in Chapter 13),
- All federal and state-required securities filings for stock issuances to founders (generally not applicable for issuance to the founders), and
- Any stock option or issuance plans and agreements.

Preparing stock issuance plans with vesting rights or stock option agreements can be quite complicated. It is advisable to consult a business attorney when drafting these documents.

What formal steps should the members of a partnership or LLC take with regard to issuing business equity?

In a corporation, the board of directors issues shares of stock to the shareholders in exchange for some value. In a partnership or LLC, the partners or members must vote to grant ownership interest in the business entity to a new partner or member. Ownership interest in the partnership is generally recorded in the partnership agreement. There are no individual documents evidencing ownership to be distributed to the new partner. In an LLC, ownership is generally recorded in the operating agreement and represented as an ownership unit. This unit may be physically distributed (similar to shares of stock) to the members. Often times, however, the LLC does not create certificates evidencing ownership; rather, evidence of ownership is maintained solely within the operating agreement. Within both the partnership and the LLC, the governing documents will indicate the voting procedure and requirements for issuing new business equity.

What employee and intellectual property matters should the board of directors or officers' address?

Establishing relationships with employees and securing intellectual property for the corporation are primary concerns for the newly appointed officers. Without the key employees and intellectual property driving the business activity, the company has very little value. The directors must act to secure employment contracts with officers. Officers will undertake employment contracts with key employees.

- *Note*: The officers will need to establish an employee handbook outlining the general operating procedure for employees and containing all federal employment law disclosures.

The officers must then turn to the issue of securing all intellectual property of relevance for the corporation. Remember, in startup ventures the company's intellectual property is often the most valuable asset. Founders who have worked on or participated in the creation of the intellectual property have ownership rights in that property. Those ownership rights need to be transferred to the corporation.

How does the corporation secure intellectual property rights?

The first step is to execute assignment of intellectual property agreements with the founders and anyone who worked on the creation of the intellectual property. The officers should then execute proprietary information and invention agreements with all permanent and temporary corporate employees. Any independent contractors of the company will be required to sign service agreement containing work-for-hire clauses for all work product or inventions. If relevant, employees should sign non-disclosure agreements for all trade secrets, research, and intellectual property. Securing intellectual property rights may include the officers making any patent applications or filing for federal trademark protection.

- *Note*: Within a startup, many of the activities outlined for shareholders, officers, and directors will be carried out by the same individuals. Remember that it is important for these individuals to indicate their status and authority in undertaking any of the above actions. While it is difficult, it is important to maintain corporate formalities.

CHAPTER 13: TAX PLANNING WHEN FUNDING AN ENTITY

CORPORATIONS

What tax issues arise when funding a business entity?

The salient tax issues when funding a business entity concern the transfer of property to the entity in exchange for an ownership interest, the receipt of value other than an ownership interest, and shareholder's basis in the funded business entity. Partnership-taxed entities and corporations (both C and S) vary in the tax treatment of these situations.

Does a shareholder incur a tax liability when transferring property to a corporation in exchange for equity?

IRC Section 351, a broad rule applying to corporations, generally defers from taxation any gain or loss incurred on property transferred to a corporation in exchange for stock. The requirements of IRC Section 351 are discussed below.

- *Example*: Eric decides to contribute his heavy machinery to a newly formed corporation. He paid $100,000 for the equipment, but has depreciated the equipment rapidly and his basis is now $50,000. The fair market value of the equipment is approximately $75,000. If he were to sell the equipment, he would recognize a gain on the sale. He instead contributes the property to the corporation in exchange for 100% of the stock of the corporation. Pursuant to IRC Section 351, Eric will not recognize a gain on the transfer of the equipment to the corporation. Likewise, pursuant to IRC Section 1032, the corporation will not pay any gain upon receipt of the equipment (discussed below).

- *Note*: Shareholders may wish to transfer property with a fair market value that is less than the basis in the asset (i.e., a loss asset). Generally, IRC Section 351 does not allow for the recognition of losses on property transferred to the corporation. In order to recognize the losses on the transaction, the shareholders should transfer the loss assets in a transaction that does not qualify for deferral of IRC Section 351. Note, however, loss recognition is not allowed if the shareholder owns (or constructively owns) more than 50% of the corporation's outstanding stock after the transaction. Alternatively, the shareholder could sell the asset, recognize the loss, and transfer the proceeds of the sale to the corporation.

Does a corporation incur a tax liability when receiving property in exchange for equity?

Generally, no. IRC Section 1032 excludes the recognition of any gain or loss on property by a corporation upon receiving property in exchange for equity.

- *Example*: In the case of Eric above, pursuant to IRC Section 1032, the corporation will not pay any gain upon receipt of the equipment.

What are the requirements to defer tax liability when transferring property to a corporation?

IRC Section 351 has several requirements. First, it only applies to the exchange of property for voting stock in the corporation. If any shareholder involved in the transaction receives equity for services or something other than voting stock, the transaction may not qualify for tax deferral. Second, following the transaction, the individuals transferring property to the corporation must control 80% of the total voting stock and 80% of each class of stock.

- *Example*: Alice, Cindy, and Jan transfer equipment to a new corporation. Each founder receives an equal portion of common stock of the corporation. The corporation does not issue a second class of stock or other security instrument. After the transaction, the three own 100% of the only class of stock of the corporation. The transaction qualifies under IRC Section 351, and the shareholder do not recognize gain on the transfer.

- *Note*: If a single shareholder runs afoul of the IRC Section 351 requirements, the benefits may be lost for all of the shareholders participating in the transaction.

Can shareholder lose the tax deferment benefit when transferring property to a corporation?

This rule has numerous limitations to further protect against sham transfers that would otherwise violate the rule. The following shareholder action can forfeit the tax deferral benefit:

- *Voting Class of Stock* - As previously stated, following the transaction, shareholders transferring property to the corporation in exchange for equity must control 80% of all existing classes of stock. This includes non-voting stock, such as preferred shares. In that sense, shareholders involved in the transaction must make certain to identify and calculate ownership percentage for each stock class.

- *Minimum Participation* - For existing corporations, existing shareholders must take part in the property transfer to meet the 80% ownership requirements of IRC Section 351. To make certain that existing shareholders do not nominally participate (i.e., play a minimal role in the transaction to allow other shareholders to satisfy IRC Section 351 requirements), existing shareholders participating in the transaction must contribute property with a value equal to at least 10% of the total value of the stock owned by those existing shareholders.

  - *Example*: Tom, Al, and Mary are equal owners of 100% of the only class of shares of Small Corp, Inc. Smith wants to become a shareholder and wishes to exchange equipment for an ownership interest in the corporation. In exchange for his contribution, Smith wants to receive 10% of the post-contribution shares. This will dilute Tom, Al, and Mary to 90% owners. Unless Tom, Al, and Mary take part in the transaction (i.e., provide additional property in exchange for shares of stock) then IRC Section 351 will not apply. To meet the IRC Section 351 requirements, Tom, Al, and Mary must contribute property equaling 10% of the total value of their ownership interest along with Smith's contribution. This will allow Smith to be part of the group owning 80% or more of the corporation immediately following the transfer.

- *Immediate Disposition of Corporate Stock* - If the corporation immediately sells or transfers property transferred to the corporation for stock, this action can forfeit the IRC Section 351 benefits for shareholders. This situation makes it appear that shareholders transferred property to the corporation as a funnel to avoid personally recognizing gains or losses associated with personally selling the property. This may be advantageous, as the corporation may have a lower tax rate or be able to offset any gains or losses on the property.

What is the result if the shareholder receives some form of value in addition to corporate shares?

IRC Section 351 permits a shareholder to contribute property and receive some form of value in addition to corporate shares. Additional value received is commonly known as "boot". The shareholder, however, will have tax liability for the non-stock value received from the corporation. Specifically, the shareholder will recognize a gain in the transaction equal to the lesser of the fair market value of the additional value received or the "built-in-gains" in the property transferred to the corporation by the shareholder. The shareholder cannot recognize losses on property transferred to the corporation.

- *Example*: Tim transfers equipment to the corporation that has a basis of $100,000 and a fair market value of $200,000. He receives a 10% stock interest in the corporation valued at $100,000 and $100,000 in cash. In this case, Tim will recognize a gain of $100,000 on the transfer of property, which is the fair market value of the boot ($100,000) and the amount of built-in-gains in the property ($100,000). If, instead of $100,000 in cash, Tim had received property from the corporation that had a fair market value of $90,000, he would have recognized gain of $90,000 (the fair market value of the boot received), which is less than $100,000 (the built-in gains in the property).

- *Note*: Types of additional value received by a shareholder include, cash, notes, bonds, non-voting securities, etc.

What is the shareholder's basis in the stock following the transfer?

Pursuant to IRC Section 358, the shareholder's basis in the corporate stock will equal the basis in the property transferred to the corporation, plus any gain that the shareholder recognizes in the transaction, minus the fair market value of any boot received from the corporation. This is known as a "substitute basis". If, however, the property transferred to the corporation has a fair market value of less than the shareholder's basis in the property, IRC Section 362(e) limits the ability of the shareholder and the corporation to recognize a loss on the transaction. In this case, the corporation and shareholders can agree on the allocation of basis. Further, rather than the shareholder maintaining a basis equal to her basis in the property transferred, the parties can agree that the basis in the newly acquired stock will equal the fair market value of the property transferred to the corporation. In this case, the corporation's basis in the newly acquired property will equal the shareholder's basis prior to transfer.

- *Example*: Michelle transfers equipment to the corporation in exchange for stock and a $1,000 computer. Her basis in the equipment is $10,000. The $1,000 computer received by Michelle is boot, which she will recognize as gain. Generally, her basis in the stock will be $10,000 ($10,000 basis + $1,000 gain recognized - $1,000 boot received). If the equipment transferred to the corporation was worth only $8,000, Michelle cannot recognize the $2,000 loss on the equipment at the time of transfer. The shareholder and corporation can, however, agree that Michelle will take an $8,000 basis (the FMV of the property) in the stock and the corporation's basis in the property will be $10,000 (the shareholder's prior basis in the equipment). As such, Michelle takes a lower basis and the corporation gets the stepped up basis.

What is the corporation's basis in the property following the transfer?

Pursuant to IRC Section 358, the corporation's basis in the property following the IRC Section 351 transaction equals the shareholder's basis in the contributed property, plus any gain recognized by the shareholder in the transaction. If the fair market value of the property transferred to the corporation is less than the shareholder's basis in the transferred property, the corporation's basis will equal the fair market value of the stock. As stated above, an exception to this rule is where the corporation and shareholder agree that the shareholder's basis in the stock will not be higher than the fair market value of the stock. This effectively places the lower basis value on the shareholder. The corporation's basis will then be the shareholder's basis in the property at the time of the transaction.

- *Example*: Donna transfers equipment with a basis of $3,000 and a fair market value of $5,000 to the corporation in exchange for stock. Assume the transaction qualifies under IRC Section 351. The corporation will take Donna's basis in the equipment, which is $3,000. If Donna elects to recognize $2,000 in gain, then the corporation's basis in the property would be $5,000. If the fair market value of the equipment at the time of transfer is $2,000 (rather than $5,000), the corporation would have a $2,000 basis and the shareholder's basis in the stock received would be her original basis of $3,000. Donna and the corporation may agree, however, to allocate the higher basis of $3,000 to the property and Donna will take a basis in the stock equal to the fair market value of the equipment ($2,000).

What happens if the corporation assumes shareholder debt associated with the transferred property?

IRC Section 351 allows for the assumption by the corporation of shareholder debt associated with property transferred to the corporation. Pursuant to IRC Section 357, the amount of debt assumed reduces the shareholder's basis in the property. If, however, the amount of debt assumed by the corporation exceeds the shareholder's basis in the contributed property, the amount of debt above the shareholder's basis in the property is treated as gain to the shareholder. The corporation's basis in the property is the amount of the assumed debt. A shareholder may lose the benefits of IRC Section 351 if the principle purpose of transferring the property and debt to the corporation was tax avoidance rather than a valid business purpose.

Assuming additional debt on property prior to transferring it to the corporation is evidence that there was not a valid business purpose. Lastly, if the shareholder also remains responsible for the debt that is jointly assumed by the corporation, it will not change the situation described above and will not destroy the exemption as long as the corporation is expected to pay the debt.

- *Example*: Winston transfers equipment with a value and a basis of $10,000 to the corporation. The equipment is subject to a promissory note owed to the dealer in the amount of $6,000. The corporation assumes the debt. Winston's basis in the newly acquired stock will be $4,000 ($10,000 basis - $6,000 debt assumed). If, however, Winston's basis in the property is $5,000, he will recognize a gain of $1,000 ($6,000 debt assumed - $5,000 debt shareholder basis). If Winston takes out loans against the property prior to transferring it to the corporation, it may be evidence that he was attempting to avoid the recognition of gain and gain may be imputed to him in the transaction.

- *Note*: If the shareholder transfers assets to the corporation that secures a debt, but the debt is also secured by property not transferred to the corporation, the corporation's basis in the property will be reduced by the value of the non-transferred property securing the debt to the extent of the security interest.

What happens if the equity received by the shareholder is in exchange for services to the corporation?

Providing services to a corporation in exchange for stock is generally a taxable event. Pursuant to IRC Section 83(a), the shareholder receiving the stock will be attributed with income equal to the fair market value of the stock at the time of issuance. There is an exception to this rule under IRC Section 83(b). This section allows shareholders to defer the recognition of the income until a later date if certain conditions exist. In summary, the shares awarded to the shareholder must face a "substantial risk of forfeiture". This means that there are provisions in the agreement that keeps ownership of the shares from vesting in the shareholder for a period of time. The most common type of restrictions is a stock award that is subject to vesting schedules and forfeiture provisions. This will allow the shareholder to defer recognition of the income until the substantial risk of forfeiture is no longer in place. This may occur once ownership of the shares of stock has fully vested in the shareholder. The downside is that shareholder will be taxed on the value of the stock at the time the substantial risk of forfeiture is gone. If the stock rises dramatically in value, the shareholder will face a much higher tax liability.

- *Example*: John receives stock in exchange for his services to New Corp, Inc. The stock award agreement states that ownership in a certain percentage of the shares will vest over several years. If John fails to meet certain performance levels or leaves the employ of New Corp, then all non-vested shares are forfeited. This would be sufficient to constitute a substantial risk of forfeiture. John will recognize income when the shares vest and there is no longer a risk of forfeiture in place.

How can a shareholder elect to immediately recognize as income shares that are subject to a

risk of forfeiture?

IRC Section 83(b) allows a shareholder receiving stock for services that is subject to a substantial risk of forfeiture to recognize the value of the stock as income in the year distributed. This allows the shareholder to recognize the stock as income before the stock increases in value. This is incredibly valuable for startup entrepreneurs who expect rapid growth of the corporation and value of the shares of stock. The risk associated with making an IRC Section 83(b) election is that the value of the stock will decrease, as there is no subsequent deduction allowed to the taxpayer. In such a case, the shareholder incurs income tax on the higher value.

- *Example*: Sarah agrees to work for the corporation in exchange for salary and an equity holding in the company. She will receive 1% ownership stake in the company at the end of each year for 3 years (her vesting schedule). If she leaves the company prior to the end of 3 years, all of her stock interest is forfeited back to the corporation. The contingency that Sarah stay at the company 3 years before owning her equity interest constitutes a substantial risk of forfeiture. Under IRC Section 83(a), Sarah can defer recognition of the stock award as income until the end of year 3. If, however, she chooses to recognize the stock award as income at the time that it vests (at the end of each year), she can elect to do so under IRC Section 83(b). Electing to recognize the income in the year awarded may lower her tax liability, as the stock will likely rise in value. If she waits until the end of year 3 to recognize the total value of the vested stock, she will pay income on the present value of the stock at that time.

- *Note*: Shareholders may not want or be able to pay the taxes on issues of stock for services, as she does not receive any cash along with the stock. In such a case, the shareholder may negotiate with the corporation to provide a bonus, known as a "gross up payment", to cover the taxes on the value of the stock received.

PARTNERSHIP - TAXED ENTITIES

What is the tax liability of the partnership when property is transferred to the entity in exchange for an ownership interest?

Pursuant to IRC Section 721, partners generally do not recognize gain or loss on the contribution of property to the business entity. Partnership taxed entities include partnerships and LLCs. I will refer to business owners collectively as partners.

- *Example*: Cliff transfers property to a partnership in exchange for a 30% ownership interest in the partnership. If the transaction qualifies under IRC Section 721, Cliff will not recognize a gain or loss on the transfer to the partnership.

What are the requirements for an exemption from the recognition of gains in an IRC Section 721 transaction?

IRC Section 721 is generally easier to navigate than IRC Section 351 in that there are no formal requirements for the transaction to qualify under the tax section. Particularly, the IRC Section

351 requirements that the contributing shareholders control more than 80% of the interest after the transaction and the concerns over voting versus non-voting shares are not applicable.

- *Example*: In the case of Cliff above, the transaction will likely qualify under IRC Section 721. If Cliff had transferred the property to a corporation, the transaction would have failed to qualify as an IRC Section 351 transaction. Cliff would not have control of more than 80% of the corporation following the transaction and would therefore have to recognize any gain or loss on the transfer.

What is the partner's basis in the ownership interest following the transfer?

Under IRC Section 722, the partner's basis in the partnership acquired in exchange for property contributed to the partnership in an IRC Section 721 transaction equals the partner's basis in the contributed property, plus any gain recognized. This is known as "outside basis".

- *Example*: In the case of cliff above, Cliff's basis in the partnership will equal his basis in the property contributed to the partnership. If Cliff's basis in the property is lower than the value of the partnership interest received, Cliff may be able to recognize a gain on the transaction. Any recognition of gain will raise Cliff's basis in the partnership by that amount.

What is the partnership's basis in the property following the transfer?

Pursuant to IRC Section 723, the partnership assumes the basis of the transferring partner in the subject property, increased by any gain recognized by the partner in the transaction. This is known as the "inside basis". Unlike IRC Section 351, IRC Section 721 does not place limits on the ability to transfer property with a loss to the entity; however, the partner's basis in the partnership can never go below zero.

- *Example*: In the case of Cliff above, the Partnership's basis will equal Cliff's basis in the property at the time of transfer. If Cliff recognizes gain on the transaction, the partnership's inside basis in the property will consist of Cliff's basis, plus the gain Cliff recognizes on the transaction.

What is the result if a partner receives some form of value in addition to an ownership interest?

Unlike IRC Section 351, IRC Section 721 does not permit the transfer of boot in the transfer of property to a partnership in exchange for an ownership interest. If a partner transfers property to a partnership in exchange for an ownership interest, the entire transaction will be treated as if it were a sale of the property to the partnership. Notably, in such a situation, the partner may recognize a loss on property transferred to the partnership. Loss recognition on the transaction is not available, however, if the partner is a 50% or more owner of the partnership (this includes a holder of a 50% or great earnings interest). Further, if the property transferred to the partnership is something other than a capital asset or is a depreciable asset, then any gain recognized by the partner owning more than 50% in the transaction will be taxed as ordinary income.

- *Example*: Garth transfers equipment to the partnership with a basis of $5,000 and a fair market value of $7,000. This transaction would qualify under IRC Section 721 and there is no recognition of gain. If, however, the partnership transfers a partnership interest worth $5,000 and a computer worth $2,000, the entire transaction will be treated as a sale of the property to the partnership. The transfer of the equipment will be treated as a sale and Garth will recognize a gain of $2,000 ($7,000 sale - $5,000 basis).

What happens if the partnership assumes shareholder debt associated with the transferred property?

The partnership may assume debt along with the transfer of property to the partnership. If the assumption of debt reduces the partner's obligation then the partnership's assumption of debt is treated as a payment of cash to the partner to the extent of her debt reduction. This lowers the partner's basis. If the debt assumed is greater than the partner's basis, she is taxed on the difference as a gain as if the property were sold for the amount of the assumed debt.

- *Example*: Victoria contributes property to the partnership with a basis of $5,000 in exchange for an interest in the partnership. The value of the property is $10,000 and there is an outstanding loan on the property of $10,000. The partnership assumes the $10,000 loan as part of the transfer of ownership. Victoria will recognize a gain on the transfer of $5,000. Victoria's basis in the partnership will be $0 ($5,000 original basis - $5,000 debt assumed).

What happens if the partner contributes property to the partnership with gain that is later sold by the partnership?

As previously stated, the partnership's basis in property received from a partner is the same as the partner's basis. If the fair market value of the property is higher than the partner's basis, then the gain in the value of the asset is not recognized. The partnership, however, must track the basis in the property for tax purposes. If the partnership later sells the property, it will have to report any amount of the sale above the basis in the property. The contributing partner is allocated gain to the extent of the built-in-gain of the asset at the time the partner transferred it to the corporation. The tricky part of this situation is that the partnership may depreciate certain property each year. As previously stated, if property is sold for higher than the basis, the gain will be attributed to the contributing partner to the extent of the built-in-gain at the time of transferring it to the corporation. Due to the depreciation of the asset, the amount of gain attributable to the partner equals the depreciated book value minus the depreciated tax basis.

- *Example*: Property with value of $300 and basis of $100 is contributed. The inside tax basis is $100. The contributing partner's inside built-in gain is $200 ($300 FMV - $100 basis). First year book value depreciation is $30 and tax basis depreciation is $10 (both are 10% of total). If the property is sold next year for $280, the total gain on the sale is $190 (280 sale price - 90 tax basis). Contributing partner's internal basis is $180 ($270 Book Value – $90 tax basis). Of the total gain, $180 is attributed to contributing partner.

The other $10 of gain is distributed equally among all partners.

What happens if property contributed to the partnership is later distributed to other partners?

If property contributed by a partner is later distributed to a non-contributing partner, it is treated as having been sold for its fair market value. This is true if the property is distributed within 7 years of the date it is contributed to the partnership. As in the above situation, any gain on the property will be attributed to the contributing partner to the extent of her built-in gain.

- *Example*: Bernice contributes property with a basis of $500 and a fair market value of $700 to the partnership. Bernice's built-in-gains in the partnership is $200. If the property is later distributed to a partner for $800, the first $200 of gain is attributed to Bernice. The remaining $100 gain is distributed equally among the partners.

How do partnerships allocate losses on the sale of property with a built-in-gain?

If property with a fair market value that is higher than the partner's basis is contributed to the partnership, the partner has a built-in gain. If the partnership later sells the property for an amount that is less than the book value (fair market value at time of contribution - depreciation), then there is a book loss to the partnership. There is, however, still a recognizable gain to the original partner if the sale price is above the partner's tax basis. In this situation, there are two ways to allocate the gains and losses. First, the entire gain (sale price - tax basis) can be attributed to the contributing partner. In this situation, the book loss is ignored. Second, the entire built-in gain in the property can be attributed to the contributing partner (book value - tax basis). This amount will also equal the realized gain, plus the amount of book losses. Since the contributing partner pays taxes on the entire amount, the book losses can be distributed to the other partners.

- *Example 1*: Thomas, a partner, contributes property worth $300 with $100 basis to the partnership. The partnership's inside basis is $100 equal to Thomas' basis at the time of contribution. After one year of depreciation (10% annual depreciation rate), the book value of the property is down to $270 and the tax basis is down to $90. That year, the property is sold for $240. This yields a gain of $150 ($240 sale price - $90 inside tax basis). The entire $150 of gain is attributed to Thomas, who has a built-in gain of $180 ($270 book value - $90 tax basis).

- *Example 2*: In the above scenario, the sale of the property yields a gain of $150, but a book loss of $30 ($270 book value - $240 sale price). If the property were sold at book value, the total gain would have been $180 ($270 book value - $90 tax basis). In such a situation, the partners may choose to allocate the entire $180 hypothetical gain to the contributing partner and split up the $30 loss between all partners.

What happens if the equity received by the partner is in exchange for services to the partnership?

As discussed in Chapter 4, when a partner receives an ownership interest in exchange for services to the business, the partner is taxed on the value of the fair market value of the partnership interest received. This situation gives rise to "phantom income", as the new partner does not actually receive any cash for her services. The partnership may award an interest that is subject to a vesting schedule and a substantial risk of forfeiture. The partner does not recognize income until the substantial risk of forfeiture is gone. If the partner wishes to recognize the value of the partnership interest as income at the time that it vests, she can make an IRC Section 83(b) election. This provision functions identically as in the corporation scenario.

- *Example*: Venus performs services to the partnership and receives a 10% partnership interest in exchange. The value of the partnership is $100,000. Venus will be taxed on the $100,000, even though she did not actually receive any funds. Venus may receive the ownership interest on a vesting schedule with forfeiture provisions if Venus leaves the partnership for any reason. As such, she will pay taxes on the value of the interest at the time it vests.

- *Note*: Unlike IRC Section 351 applicable to corporations, the distribution of equity for services as part of a IRC Section 721 transaction involving the contribution of property does not destroy the ability to defer the recognition of gain or loss on the contribution.

- *Note*: Rather than giving an ownership interest to individuals providing services to the business, partnership often award a profits interest in the business. A profits interest is a contractual right to share in the profits of the partnership pursuant to the terms of the profits interest agreement. The notable difference between an ownership interest and a profits interest is that the profits interest does not entail the other rights and liabilities associated with ownership.

CHAPTER 14: CONVERTING ENTITIES

What is the process to convert from one entity status to another?

The answer depends upon the technique used to convert and the type of entity from which the business is converting. With the exception of changing from S to C corporation status (and vice versa), converting from one business entity to another requires the organizer to undertake the steps previously discussed in Chapters 5 -through 9 to form a new business entity. The techniques for converting generally include liquidating the existing entity or merging the existing entity into the new entity.

What are the options in converting from a partnership or LLC (partnership) to a corporate entity status?

As stated above, conversion from a partnership to a corporate status can be done by liquidating (dissolving) the current business entity or by transferring ownership of the current entity over to the corporation. Here is a breakdown of the options:

- <u>Liquidation Option</u> - Liquidation requires the partnership to wind down operations, distribute its assets, and dissolve the entity. Distributing assets can be done in two ways. First, after paying off all liabilities, the partnership can distribute the remaining assets to the partners. The partners are then free to undertake the process necessary to organize the new entity. This may include contributing the assets received from the liquidation of the partnership (cash and property) to the new corporate entity. Second, the partnership may liquidate by contributing partnership assets to the new corporate entity. The partnership receives corporate stock for the contribution. The partnership is then dissolved and the corporate stock assets are distributed to the partners.

    - *Note*: The second method is not available if the new corporation elects S status. Remember, all owners of an S corporation must be real people. The partnership cannot own an interest in the S corporation without jeopardizing its S status.

- <u>Merger Option</u> - The new corporation acquires the ownership interest of the partners in exchange for an ownership interest in the new corporation. The result is that the new corporation owns the partnership and all of its assets. The corporation can then wind up the affairs of the partnership in the manner most advantageous to the corporation. This could include transferring contracts, property, and other assets. The partnership becomes one with the new corporation.

Do partners recognize any gain or loss in the conversion from a partnership to a corporate entity?

The partners will recognize any gain or loss following the liquidation of partnership property. That is, if the proceeds from the liquidation of partnership assets exceed the partner's basis in the partnership, then there will be a taxable gain. Likewise, if the proceeds from the liquidation are less than the partner's basis in the partnership, the partner will recognize a loss in the conversion. If the partnership merges with the new corporation, the partners will have contributed property to the corporation in exchange for stock. As discussed in Chapter 13, IRC Section 351 may apply to defer the recognition of any gain or loss on property when contributing any assets and liabilities to the new corporation.

- *Example*: Terrence and Mike are partners. Each contributes property with a value of $10,000 in exchange for his partnership interest. When the partnership liquidates its assets, it receives $22,000. Terrence and Mike will have a taxable gain on the liquidation of $1,000 each. If the partnership interest is contributed directly to the corporation, the transaction may qualify under IRC Section 351 to defer the recognition of gain by the partners.

- *Note*: The liquidation of assets by the partnership may lead to a gain or loss for the partners contributing that asset.

Does the partnership recognize any gain or loss in the conversion from a partnership to a corporate entity?

If the partnership liquidates its assets, it will recognize any gains or losses on those assets if sold to outside individuals. The partnership will not recognize any gains or losses if it simply distributes the assets or liabilities to its partners. Remember, the tax basis of the partners contributing any property to a partnership is tracked for tax purposes. As previously discussed, gain on property sold, transferred, or distributed by the partnership may give rise to a gain for the contributing partner. Pursuant to IRC Section 358, if the partnership transfers the assets and liabilities to the new corporation, then it may not recognize any gain or loss. In such a transaction, a partnership's basis in the stock received equals the basis in the assets and there is no taxable gain or loss to the partnership. The partnership may face gains or losses when the internal assets are liquidated.

- *Example*: Anne and Carl are partners of Anne's Place. Anne's Place contributes all of it's assets to Big, Inc., in exchange for shares of Big, Inc. Anne's Place may defer recognition of gain or loss on the transaction. Anne and Carl, however, may incur gains or losses upon distribution of the partnership assets.

What will be the partner's basis in the new corporation?

Each partner's basis in the assets distributed to the partner by the partnership will equal the partner's basis in the partnership. So, if those assets are then contributed to a corporate entity, the partner's basis in the new entity is unchanged. If the assets are liquidated by the partnership and transferred to the new corporation in exchange for stock of the new corporation, the partnership's basis in the stock is equal to the value transferred to the corporation for the stock. If the assets and liabilities of the partnership are simply transferred to the corporation (rather than sold and the proceeds transferred), the partnership's basis in the corporate stock will equal the partnership's basis in the assets and liabilities transferred. When the partnership dissolves and distributes the stock, the partner's basis will equal the partner's basis in the partnership, plus any gain or loss recognized on the distribution. If the corporation assumes any liabilities that reduce the liability of the partner, the partner's basis in stock received is reduced accordingly. If the partnership and corporation merge, the partners' basis in the stock will equal their basis in the partnership interest contributed to the corporation.

What is the new corporation's basis in assets contributed by the partners or partnership?

If the partners or partnership transfers assets to the corporation, the corporation's basis in those assets equals the partners' or partnership's basis. If the partnership transfers assets to the corporation in exchange for stock, and the partners' basis in the partnership is higher than the partnership's basis in the internal assets, the corporation takes the lower partnership basis. The partner's basis in the stock equals the partners' basis in the property. If, however, the partnership is merged into the corporation, the corporation takes the partners' outside basis as the basis of the partnership assets when the partnership is liquidated.

What does it take to convert from S to C corporation status?

The decision to become an S corporation is nothing more than a tax election. Therefore, if the entity meets the requirements to be an S corporation, the act of converting to a C corporation is very simple. To begin the conversion process, more than 50% of the corporate shareholders must vote to make a Subchapter S election. The S corporation board must then vote to approve the decision to convert to a C corporation. The corporation must then execute the appropriate IRS form.

- *Note*: An S corporation can lose its S election status by failing to adhere to S corporation requirements. If so, the C corporation cannot return to S status within a 5-year period without permission from the IRS.

What are the tax consequences of converting from S to C corporation status?

As previously discussed, C corporation income is subject to a double tax structure. Any retained earnings of the S corporation that are distributed to shareholders within one year of conversion to a C corporation will be tax free and will reduce the shareholder's basis in the C corporation to the extent of the S corporation's accumulated earnings account.

- *Note*: This one-year period allows shareholders a period to withdraw funds accrued as an S corporation.

What does it take to convert from C corporation status to a partnership or LLC?

Converting from a C corporation status to a partnership-taxed entity requires that the corporation be liquidated. This generally gives rise to extensive tax consequences due to the built-in-gains of corporate assets.

- *Note*: Upon liquidation, the corporation will pay tax at ordinary income rates on the value of the assets above the adjusted basis. Further, shareholders will pay capital gains tax on any distributions above the shareholder's basis in the stock.

What does it take to convert from C to S corporation status?

To convert from C to S corporation status requires that the corporation meet the numerous requirements to be an S corporation. As stated in Chapter 9, to qualify for S corporation status, the business must be a corporation organized in the United States. All shareholders must be U.S. Citizens or resident aliens. It cannot have more than 100 shareholders. All members of a family are considered to be one investor for purposes of this rule. All shareholders must be individuals, trusts, or certain other exempt organizations. The company may only authorize one class of stock (common stock). The company must follow an accepted tax year. Finally, all shareholders must consent to the S-Election. The corporation must meet all of these requirements on the first day of the year in which the tax election is effective. 100% of the shareholders must vote to convert to S status. The board must then authorize the filing.

- *Note*: All shareholders who owned an interest in the C corporation during the tax year of election must also agree to the conversion. This includes individuals who no longer own shares in the corporation.

When is the S election effective?

There are multiple options for when the S election becomes effective. The application may request that the election become effective on a specific date. This splits the annual tax year for the corporation into two tax years. The portion of the year prior to the S election is taxed as a C corporation. The tax year after the election is taxed as an S corporation. If the corporation fails to request a specific effective date, then the default rules for the taxable year apply. If the corporation makes the election prior to the 15th day of the third month of the year, then the election is effective for the year of election. If the election is made after this date, the election will become effective during the following tax year.

What are the tax consequences when converting from C to S corporation status?

Any profits that remain in the corporation after the effective date of the S election will be treated as a dividend to shareholders if these funds are distributed. Any future earnings after the effective date of the S election will pass through to the shareholders. Any assets of the C corporation that are sold after the S-Election will be subject to a corporate gains tax and will be treated as a dividend to the shareholders.

- *Note*: Remember, the C corporation must meet all of the requirements of an S corporation at the time of election.

CHAPTER 15: WHEN TO INCORPORATE

This chapter discusses an entrepreneur's timing considerations for when to incorporate her startup venture. I use the terms incorporate and incorporation generally to refer to the decision to form a separate entity (other than a sole proprietorship or GP) for the business activity. Entrepreneurs may put off incorporating until business operations are established or there is adequate capital in place. Below are some considerations or factors to use when determining when to incorporate.

How can incorporating early help avoid disputes with other founders?

An important point that the world learned from Mark Zuckerberg regards the value of formally establishing roles and ownership interests early in the life of a business. You may recall that the Winklevoss brothers sued Zuckerberg in a highly publicized trial to determine their ownership interest in the business organization. The brothers claimed an ownership interest in Facebook, Inc., based upon their alleged contributions to the venture early in its formation. This scenario goes to show that, as a general rule, a startup should incorporate when there is more than one founder. Part of the problem results from the fact that founders are renowned for making loose promises of equity ownership to those assisting in the early stages of the business. These promises often result in later disputes and lawsuits. Incorporating forces (or at least encourages) the founders to formally establish the authority and ownership interest of each founder.

- *Note*: Stock distribution agreements with founders and early employees should always include repurchase rights for vested shares and forfeiture of unvested shares.

When should I incorporate to limit personal liability?

As previously discussed, incorporating protects individuals from personal liability for the debts of the corporation. Carrying out business operations necessarily entails entering into contractual agreements with third parties. Failure to comply with any of these agreements can lead to liability for the parties. Incorporating allows the founders to enter into agreements in the name of the corporation, rather than their names. Founders must take care to maintain corporate formalities in order avoid the loss of liability protection.

- *Note*: When entering into agreements prior to incorporating a business entity, founders should identify themselves in the role of incorporator.

Should I incorporate before hiring employees?

As discussed in prior chapters, an employee is an agent of the business. Carrying on any sort of business activity prior to incorporating defaults into a sole proprietorship or GP. Therefore, an employee of the business activity subjects the founder(s) to personal liability for her tortious actions within the scope of employment. Incorporating before hiring employees eases the process. The business can file for an EIN and state taxpayer identification number and set up withholding and deposit requirements. Lastly, incorporating allows the issuance of equity to founders, employees, investors, etc. Recall that founder and early-employee, stock agreements will often be subject to a vesting schedule or include restricted stock options.

- *Note*: Early in the life of a business, compensating individuals with stock options is a common manner of acquiring talent without sufficient capital to pay a salary.

How does timing affect business intellectual property?

The early creation of intellectual property by founders is a huge issue. If the business activity involves intellectual property, the founders should incorporate as soon as possible and transfer ownership in the intellectual property to the business. Any improvements or modifications to the intellectual property will therefore inhere in the business. Failure to do so could give rise to disputes between the parties regarding the ownership of the property if one party leaves the business at a later date. In any event, business owners should use work-for-hire agreements to make certain that the work and creations of employees and contractors are the legal property of the business.

- *Example*: Jake and Elise work together to create a new design for a robot. Early in in the process, Jake breaks away form the partnership and attends college. Elise continues to work on the robot. She incorporates the business and assembles a research and development team. Years later, Elise and her team are successful in selling the robotics technology to a large corporation. Jake sues Elise and the corporation to obtain a portion of the sales proceeds. The court will have to determine the extent of Jake's interest in the business venture at the time of dissolution of the partnership. Failure by the parties to have a formal agreement regarding intellectual property rights has caused considerable controversy over who has ownership rights in the technology.

- *Note*: It is important to have comprehensive intellectual property transfer agreements that transfer all existing intellectual property rights to the corporation at or near the time of formation.

How does timing affect the tax basis for founder ownership interest?

A successful business will typically become more valuable over time as it grows. Incorporating early and transferring assets to the business creates a basis in the common shares. Stock option plans with vesting periods are used to compensate early employees. These individuals will want to establish an early basis in the stock 9when the price is lower) and pay taxes on the shares at that time. The IRS allows an employee or founder to make an IRC Section 83(b) election preserving the basis at the time of award of the stock or stock option. When the stock later vests it maintains the early basis and the employee is not taxed at the higher valuation. The shareholder pays taxes on the value of the stock options when granted. The stock will be taxed on the increased value at the time of sale. If the holding period is longer than one year, the long-term capital gain tax rate will apply, rather than the ordinary income rate.

- *Note*: Failing to make the IRC Section 83(b) election means that the shareholder will pay ordinary income taxes on the receipt of stock options at the time of vesting. If the value of the options increases from the time of granting, the holder of the option will pay higher taxes. All parties who intend to sell their interest in the business will want to take advantage of the long-term capital gain rate. Incorporating early and vesting shares in founders will begin the holding period.

- *Example*: Darlene and Wallis found a new technology startup. They immediately form a corporation and distribute 1,000 shares of founder's stock to each founder. The founder's basis in the stock will be the value of the company at the time of issuance. At this early stage of the business, the founder's basis is very low. If the founders wait until the technology assets have substantial value, then the value of shares in the company will be much higher.

How does incorporating early in the life of the startup facilitate equity financing?

As discussed in prior chapters, investors in the corporation generally require preferred shares in exchange for their investment capital. Incorporating early will signal to potential investors that the business is established and open to outside funding. Further, it makes it easier for the investors to carry out due diligence and reduces the costs associated with reforming the entity at the time of equity investment.

- *Note*: Reducing equity funding costs is a concern for the business, as the costs of funding (the investor and the corporation's attorney) are generally paid by the business. The amount is taken directly from the funds injected by the investor.

What other considerations on timing are important when incorporating?

Incorporating a business triggers all of the maintenance requirements, discussed previously. Founders should be prepared to comply with all corporate formalities. Further, if a founder is employed elsewhere, make certain that there are anti-compete clauses that would be triggered by incorporating the business. Likewise, if an employee is subject to work-for-hire provisions in an employment contract, make certain that there will not be any disputes over the ownership of intellectual property between the businesses.

- *Note*: Employees and directors (particularly those in small to medium-size businesses) are bound by a duty of loyalty to their employer. They cannot usurp a business deal for their personal interest that originates as a result of their status as employees or directors. Creating a formal business entity may expose a potential conflict of interest in dual employment status or situations where a director is also affiliated in another business in a similar industry.

CHAPTER 16: IN WHICH STATE TO INCORPORATE

A business can incorporate in any state in the United States, regardless of whether it carries on substantial business in that state. Most states simply require that the business maintain a registered agent within the state for service of process and other notification requirements. Further, this registered agent may be required to maintain certain corporate records for inquiring third parties at the agent's designated place of business. With this in mind, many businesses choose to incorporate in states other than their primary place of business. The most common state of incorporation is Delaware; however, many startups (particularly technology startups) decide to incorporate in California. Other entities incorporate in off-shore tax havens, such as the Cayman Islands, in an attempt to establish a more favorable tax structure.

Why do companies incorporate in Delaware?

Delaware is a target state for incorporation for a number of reasons. Delaware offers easy formation and maintenance procedures for companies. The main reason companies choose to incorporate in Delaware, however, regards the business law system. Delaware offers a very well developed body of corporate law. Many states mimic Delaware statutes and courts find Delaware chancery court opinions very influential. Chancery courts are business specialty courts that are presided over by a Chancellor (Judge) and do not typically allow jury trials. Businesses feel more comfortable in the chancery court as the judges are experts in corporate law. Further, the overall body of law (both common and statutory) is generally favorable to corporations and their directors (as apposed to outside plaintiffs and shareholders). Lastly, investors generally prefer to invest in Delaware corporations. The predictable body of law is the primary reason. Each of these considerations is discussed in detail below.

What are Delaware's formation and maintenance advantages?

Hundreds of corporations form or register in Delaware on a weekly basis. The Secretary of State's office is equipped to handle this high volume, so the process is fast and easy. Further, the maintenance procedures for maintaining corporate status are minimal. Generally, a company only has to file any major changes in information contained in the articles of incorporation. Any notifications can be filed electronically. Corporate meetings can be held virtually, which makes the quorum requirement easier to satisfy. Proxy votes can be cast electronically. Consents can be voted upon and signed electronically. While many states require consents to be voted upon by all shareholders, Delaware allows for consents by less than all shareholders. Unlike many other states, Delaware only requires one corporate director.

What are the advantages of Delaware's chancery courts and body of corporate law?

The Delaware chancery court is a court of equity authorized under the Delaware constitution. A chancellor (or vice chancellor) presides over hearings as a judge. The court does not employ juries, but it has the authority to assemble an advisory jury if needed. The chancellors are experts in corporate law, including aspects of securities regulation, commercial law, antitrust law, corporate governance, and other highly technical areas. Because of the large number of corporations organized under Delaware law, many of the nations most complicated corporate law issues are tried in the Delaware courts. Chancery court opinions appeal to the Delaware Supreme Court, which attempts to address important questions of corporate law expeditiously. Over the years, Delaware has developed the most comprehensive body of corporate, common law in the United States. Further, the legislature is very responsive to emergent issues in corporate law. This fact gives corporations a great deal of confidence in organizing in Delaware and drafting contracts subject to Delaware law. Businesses understand the state of the law, which reduces any ambiguity in the legal status of corporation actions.

How are Delaware laws favorable to corporations?

Corporate laws in every state require that directors act in the best interest of company shareholders. Instances where directors fail to act accordingly are the subject of shareholder derivative actions. As previously discussed, directors are protected by a doctrine known as the "business judgment rule". Decisions by directors that harm the corporation may be actionable in a derivative suit, but they can defend themselves by asserting that they used their best judgment given the circumstances. If the court believes that the director acted in good faith, used reasonable judgment, and intended to act in the corporation's best interest, she is protected from liability. Delaware is known for having a director-friendly, business judgment rule. This is a strong draw to directors of corporations. Within startups, the founders are generally the directors and executives, even if the majority of shareholders are outside investors. As with employees of a limited liability entity, a favorable business judgment rules reduces the personal risk to directors. Further, Delaware allows corporations to indemnify their directors against losses due to derivative liability. These self-serving provisions are generally proposed and approved by the directors of Delaware corporations.

What type of governance requirements attracts startups?

Another aspect of Delaware law is the reduction of formalities required in approving corporate actions. For example, Delaware is less stringent in requiring majority vote of shareholders or directors on many issues. Many actions are approved by a majority of shares voting, rather than a majority of shares outstanding. Startup ventures often intend to sell their business and merge with a strategic investor. Such an action under many states' laws requires unanimous approval by all shareholders. Delaware allows for a majority vote of shareholders in approving major corporate decisions. As such, Delaware is attractive to investors who do not want common shareholders to have the ability to block a sale or merger.

Do investors prefer Delaware corporations?

For the above-stated reasons, venture capitalists, private equity firms, and bank underwriters often prefer that startups going through a public offering organize in Delaware. They will often require a company organized in another state to re-organize in Delaware. The costs and requirements of doing so can be very burdensome on the business. For startups with the objective of rapid growth leading to an exit event, such as an IPO, this is a strong incentive to incorporate in Delaware.

What are the downsides of incorporating in Delaware?

The main downside to incorporating in Delaware, as apposed to your state of operations, is that you subject yourself to the Delaware court's jurisdiction. This means that a plaintiff can sue you in Delaware, rather than in your home state or the state where the alleged harm occurred. While this may be a desired result for many businesses, small startups that do not have a significant presence in Delaware may find it an extreme burden to defend lawsuits there. Jurisdiction and the ability to sue a business in a state are discussed further in Chapter 15.

Why do some businesses incorporate in the Cayman Islands (or other tax haven localities)?

Businesses often search for more favorable locations to incorporate for tax purpose. This is a complicated topic, but companies can allocate a portion of their earnings or expenses to functions carried out at their headquarters. When the headquarters is a location outside of the United States, the income may be considered as foreign. This income may be exempt from taxation within the U.S., and may be taxed at a lower rate than the federal and state rates.

- *Note*: A common practice with businesses that wish to avoid federal income taxation is to create captive insurance companies. Often these companies have foreign headquarters that allow for collection of premiums from the parent business free of taxation. The premiums are then invested on a pre-tax basis to the benefit of the parent corporation.

CHAPTER 17: MULTI-STATE BUSINESSES

What happens when a business wants to do business in more than one state?

A business must choose its state of formation or organization. The home state may be the location where the business is headquartered or it may be any other state where the business organizes and establishes a registered agent. If a business chooses Delaware as its state of formation, for example, it may still carry on business in another state. If the business wishes to carry on business outside of its home state, it must qualify to do business and register as a "foreign" entity doing business in the other state. A business may carry on the majority or all of its business in a state or states where it is registered as a foreign entity.

- *Example:* Vince forms a business in New York. He follows all of the applicable procedures required by the New York Secretary of State's Office. The business grows quickly and he looks to expand into Massachusetts. In order to carry on business in Massachusetts, Vince has to register his business in that state. He goes to the Massachusetts Secretary of State's website and fills out the paperwork to register as a foreign entity doing business in the state. He can then proceed to get a business license in Massachusetts. Now Vince's business may carry on activities in both New York and Massachusetts.

- *Note*: There are several important points to consider when deciding whether to incorporate in one state and file as a foreign entity in another state. First, you will have to pay annual fees in every state in which you are organized or registered. Second, carrying on business in multiple states adds complexity in calculating the business' tax liability. Third, and perhaps most importantly, the business entity may be sued (i.e., is subject to the court's jurisdiction) in any state in which it is organized or registered.

What constitutes "doing business" within a state?

Each state has its own interpretation of what constitutes "doing business" within the state. Common types of activity that qualify are:

- Selling goods,
- Providing services,
- Negotiating or consummating transactions, and
- Building or constructing things.

The physical presence of the business within the state (such as having an office or owning property) influences the determination of whether an activity constitutes "doing business". Most states determine that the following conduct does not constitute carrying on business:

- Making shipments in or though a state;
- Accepting mail, telephone, or internet order in state;
- Selling through retailers in a state; or
- Holding property ancillary to transactions, such as bank accounts or hiring professional

legal services in a state.

What happens if the laws of a state in which you wish to do business are different from the laws of the home state?

This is a common occurrence with specialty entity types. For example, some states recognize business entities that do not exist in other states, such as professional corporations, statutory close corporations, limited liability limited partnerships, etc. In general, if the foreign state does not have a commensurate business entity, the foreign business may still conduct business in that state under its home-state organizational structure. The home state's substantive laws governing the organization and maintenance of the business entity will continue to apply to the operations of the business in the foreign state. The foreign state's procedural laws regarding the registration of foreign entities within the state will also apply.

- *Note:* If the business is a defendant in a lawsuit in the foreign state, the laws of the foreign state apply to the cause of action. There is an exception, however, when the dispute involves a contract governed by the laws of another state. Commonly, businesses organize in Delaware and construct all of their contracts pursuant to the laws of that state. If sued on the contract in a foreign state, the laws of the state of Delaware are applied to the business litigation. This can also be accomplished through a "choice of law" clause in a contract.

How similar are each state's business laws?

While each state adopts is own business entity laws, most state business codes and the common law developed in that state are relatively similar. This is due in large part to model laws passed by the National Conference of Commissioners on Uniform State Laws or the American Bar Association. These model laws are not binding on any state, but serve as recommendations, guides and best practices in the formation of business entity law. Examples of these model acts includes the:

- Model Business Corporations Act,
- Uniform Partnership Act,
- Uniform Limited Partnership Act,
- Uniform Limited Liability Company Act,
- Model Entity Transactions Act,
- Uniform Franchise and Business Opportunities Act,
- Uniform Limited Cooperative Association Act,
- Model Nonprofit Corporation Act,
- Model Real Estate Cooperative Act,
- Uniform Trusts Act,
- Uniform Statutory Trust Entity Act,
- Model Multi-state Trust Institutions Act,
- Uniform Commercial Code.

Entrepreneurs or business managers should review a state's law to determine whether it has adopted the model acts.

How are multi-state businesses taxed?

In general, a business is subject to state income taxation in the state in which it earns the income. For example, a business is taxed on the income received from consummating a sale or carrying out a service in a state. The business must also pay sales tax on any sales consummated in the state if the business has a significant presence in that state. This is a hot topic for internet retailers, such as Amazon. Each state has its own rules with regard to what constitutes a significant presence.

- *Note*: Amazon has been very successful in negotiating with state governments to exempt Amazon sales from state sales tax, even if the business has a substantial presence in the state (such as a distribution facility).

How are multi-state businesses exposed to increased potential liability?

A business that carries on activity in multiple states may be subject to the jurisdiction of courts in each state. The standard for whether a business is subject to jurisdiction in a state is whether the state has "sufficient minimum contacts to not offend notions of fair play and substantial justice?" Minimum contacts is a floating standard and subject to determination by the individual court. If the business is subject to jurisdiction in multiple states, it increases the pool of potential plaintiffs. Further, it increases the burden on the business to defend itself in a variety of states.

- *Example*: Flow manufactures and sells shoes in Georgia. She is a Georgia LLC and is registered to do business in state. She decides to expand her sales to all 50 states through the internet. A customer in California buys a pair of her shoes over the internet. She ships the shoes to California. The customer claims to suffer a foot injury after wearing the shoes. The customer attempts to sue flow in California. The court will determine whether Flow has sufficient contact with the state to allow the customer to sue her in California. If the court determines that Flow has sufficient minimum contacts with California, she will have to defend the lawsuit in California. Unless the contract of sale states otherwise, the court will apply California law. If the court determines that she does not have minimum contacts with California, the customer will have to sue her in Georgia. In this way, Flow could be subject to increased potential liability by having to defend a lawsuit in the states where she does business.

- *Note*: Some states impose penalties on businesses that fail to file and register in a state before doing business. One such penalty is delaying or not allowing that business to enforce its rights in that state's court until it has registered and paid a substantial fine.

Closing Remarks

Having a base understanding of business entities will make you a stronger entrepreneur, manager, or professional practitioner. You now have a solid understanding of how business entities function and can carry on business with third parties with greater confidence. While you may require professional assistance to structure a business entity to maximize the available business benefits, you now have sufficient knowledge to recognize opportunities and to seek assistance when necessary.

Thank you choosing The Business Professor book series. Please visit www.TheBusinessProfessor.com to explore our other resources.

Sincerely,

Jason M. Gordon, JD, MBA, LLM

23072428R00071

Made in the USA
Middletown, DE
16 August 2015